Goldfield Mill—a remnant of the boom days.
Photographer Trisha Kuhl.

his knowledge of their ailments he effected many cures. These acts were looked upon with gratitude by his captors, and after a few days he was taken to a deep ravine, through which a small stream of water was running, and allowed to work the auriterous gravel for gold. He was rewarded by finding coarse gold so plentiful that in a few washings he filled his pockets with nuggets. Knowing that several bullets cut from wounded soldiers were found to be gold, and that they were in the Smithsonian Institute at Washington, he was aware that he stood upon the ground that produced these precious messengers of death. The sides of the canyon rose sheer up hundreds of feet, and he was unable to accurately locate the spot, though he could see in the distance the crest of a huge peak known as Weaver's Needle.

Soon after Surgeon Brayton escaped and after many hardships reached Fort Yuma, where he exhibited the golden nuggets and described the great treasure in the Tonto range. The occurrence caused intense excitement and several unsuccessful expeditions explored the region headed by Surgeon Brayton, who, strange to say, could not locate the diggings. It was always supposed that the gold came from the Adams region, but this was disproved during the last year.

The theory now advanced is that the treasure lies south of the San Juan region, at present creating much excitement and an expedition has entered the Tonto mountains from the north, taking as its guide the continuation southward from the San Juan district. It is conceded by old miners that if the country of "golden bullets" is discovered, it will develop one of the greatest placer districts ever opened in the west.

Over 1000 pounds of stolen Goldfield ore hidden in the Superstitions

By
Helen Corbin

FOXWEST PUBLISHING

Acknowledgments

Tom Kollenborn—Curator, Superstition Mountain Historical Society & Geologist

Bob Corbin—President of the National Rifle Association of America

Gregory Davis—Directory of Research and Acquisitions, Superstition Mountain Historical Society

Cover nuggets courtesy of Elaine Schrader, Pro Mack South

Nancy Sawyer—Archives Assistant, Department of Library and Archives of the State of Arizona

Charles Crismon—Director, Farm & Heritage Museum, Mesa, Arizona

Mike Meyer—History Director, National Archives, Washington, D.C.

Ron Livingston—Director, Family History Center, Mesa, Arizona

Carol Nance—Assistant Attorney General, State of Virginia

John Swarengin—Historian, Florence, Arizona

Della A.R. Meadows—Medical Historian, Pinal County, Arizona

Ileen D. Snoddy—Director, Salt River Project History Services

Arizona Historical Society, Tucson, Arizona

University of Arizona Library, Tucson, Arizona

Richard Moses-Hayden Collection—Arizona State University Library

Taylor Welch—First American Title Insurance Agency of Yavapai Inc.

American Cattleman's Association

Yavapai County Historical Society

Robin Fox & Associates—Graphic Design

Trishia Kuhl—Cover Photographs

Christina Edelblat—Editor

SENNER'S GOLD

ISBN 1-879029-02-2

Graphics/Production: Robin Fox & Associates

0 9 8 7 6 5 4 3 2 1

Library of Congress Catalog Number: 93-073213

For information contact the Publisher:

Foxwest Publishing
2834 North 29th Street
Suite 1
Phoenix, AZ 85008

PUBLISHED IN THE UNITED STATES OF AMERICA

Dedication

To treasure seekers
everywhere.

Table of Documents, Maps and Photographs

Table of Contents

From the Author

Our story is centered around the town of Goldfield in the Arizona Territory which came to life in November of 1892 when the first claim in the area was filed. The original mine, the Black Queen, trumpeted the cry of gold throughout the West and soon, as many a sixty-five other claims had been filed. The most famous of these was the Mammoth Mine, whose Mormon Stope bore the mother lode. It is said over two million dollars in ore was removed from the Mormon Stope alone, which today would be worth some 32 million dollars. A pair of Denver entrepreneurs named Sullivan and Hall bought the claim for $20,000.00. Having made their fortunes in mines in Leadville, Colorado, both men were familiar with the game and Goldfield became a big operation quickly. Before they were finished there were many miles of tunnels and miners were working down as far as 1000 feet beneath the desert floor.

Geologically the principal ore body, the Mormon Stope, was located in the area of two northward striking and steeply westward dipping faults which outcropped about three hundred feet apart. In this vicinity the richest ore was produced from granite outcroppings heavily stained with brownish limonite containing stringers of quartz which was oxidized and changed by heat. Iron pyrite within the quartz was the gold bearing iron-oxide. The rich body of ore had been split by a fault millions of years before. On the surface only small amounts of gold were found, but at 65 feet a large deposite showed up and between seventy and two hundred and fifty feet the gold was so rich it held the quartz matrix together in the stamp mill. It became difficult for the mine to separate it.

Instantly a town was born which was officially a five hour horse ride from Mesa City and was just off the route traveled between Fort MacDowell and Pinal. It grew out of need and soon enjoyed a reputation as the toughest in the Territory. Most estimates put the population at around fifteen hundred people in the area when the mines were running at capacity. There was never any law in Goldfield; 'Frontier Justice' prevailed. Two huge cottonwood trees at nearby Government Wells served the vigilantes when needed. Although Goldfield had its inception in 1892, it was dead by 1896, just four years after the boom started. It shuddered a few times after that, when stalwarts with money and hope tried to resurrect it, but for all intents and purposes it remained dead. Goldfield became a ghost town—eventually succumbing to blowing dust, rolling tumbleweeds and the springs seeping into a labyrinth of tunnels. The water ultimately formed a huge natural pond. The entire place is shadowed by a spectacular mesa called Superstition Mountain in the giant range known by the same name.

* * *

Early in the 1950's during geologist, historian Tom Kollenborn's youth, his father was injured in an automobile accident. Because of George Kollenborn's career as an engineer with the Army, he was sent to Fort Whipple Veteran's Hospital in Prescott, Arizona for treatment. The family rented a house on Washington Street for the summer. Young Tom used the time to read, scout the cool, lush area and mow lawns for neighbors to earn money. While his father recovered, both Tom and George spent time with a neighbor named Katie. The elderly woman became a favorite. Not only did Katie pay Tom $2.00 a week to mow her lawn, but she amused them with stories of a lost Superstition treasure and of two men whom she loved. The senior Kollenborn wrote all of the information into his diary. George and Tom Kollenborn spent a great deal of their time in the Superstitions. Dutchman hunting was already an avocation for George, that fact was well known, and mining was his career. Tom recalls the time and the stories, but wishes now, he had paid more attention to detail.

It seems a cowboy-miner, one Al Senner, highgraded over 1000 pounds of cobbed Goldfield ore and secreted it in deer-skin pouches on the top of Superstition Mountain. Senner's motive was the love of a lady named Katie. Their story, and the doctor who befriended both of them, makes for fascinating reading and provides treasure hunters with one more legend involving the now infamous Superstition Mountains.

* * *

Recently, this author discussed writing a novel based on what facts were available with a well known western publisher, Mark Harris. When it was stated the story begged to be told but couldn't be documented in every situation, Mark said, "That is what we call FACTION." Here then is. . . SENNER'S GOLD, a factional account of a true treasure story.

Chapter 1

The Ten Dollar Gold Piece

Senner had never thought about gold. He was a cowboy—plain and simple. And just yesterday that had seemed to be enough, yet, here he was blowing away the only life he had ever known to go search for treasure. He clucked at Lady to spur her on, staring absently at the giant Superstition Mountain Range which seemed endless from his vantage point, and which was at least a day's ride away from Phoenix in the Arizona Territory.

The February sun warmed him and was comforting. He pulled down the brim of the stained brown felt, squinting into the new day and turning slightly, glanced back at the mule following on a lead. They were headed to a small valley near the mountains where the Apaches lived. That thought brought on a hard glare. Senner knew it could be dangerous there but it was the only place known where he might strike it rich. He reflected on a recent conversation with Luke, a fellow cowhand on McKenny's ranch. They were headed to town, it was Saturday last.

Luke said, "Are you serious, Al? You don't know nothin' but punchin' cows. Okay, so you and the old man don't get on-so. He ain't around all the time and it's steady pay, decent grub and a bed. What else is there?"

Senner, a loner by nature, had declined to answer. He was certainly not going to tell his friend that he'd met the most beautiful woman ever in Mesa City. He was not going to admit he was smitten and he was not going to tell this young cowboy that she had said something to him so powerful it could not be forgotten. And, all the while that Luke talked on, Senner kept hearing her voice echo in his head.

Katie's answer to his proposal had been, "Oh! no, Mr. Senner. I've been proposed to by every drifter, cowpoke, miner and sodbuster in the territory and you are no different. I've decided not to be poor the rest of my life. I have no intention of winding up with a passel of kids and no money, trying to scrape food off the dust of the prairie and getting old before my time because of it. The man who gives me his name must also give me a good life."

In his mind's eye Senner could still see her face. God! she was beautiful. Her hair was the color of a sorrel mare he'd once had, and her eyes looked a little deeper than palo verde bark; she had milk white skin, and her rosy lips opened into a smile that just twanged at his heart. He guessed he'd never felt like this in his life. When he stood beside her the smell of her scented soap lingered in his nostrils which were above the top of the knot of her hair. He felt as though he could just scoop her smallness up into his arms and carry her away where he'd make her safe forever. Gritting his teeth he'd muttered, "Don't fret none, Katie, I'll get what I need to have you."

Luke's voice droned on. They ate a steak at the hotel restaurant and headed toward the bar where a Faro game was in progress. Senner's long, lean frame sauntered toward it. He ordered two beers. Luke followed and leaned heavily on the bar-rail while one of the dance hall girls tried to entice him. Suddenly, as if a decision had been reached, Senner pulled out a ten dollar gold piece and twisted it in front of Luke's startled eyes.

"Where'd you get that?" the cowboy questioned.

Senner grinned. "Helped a sodbuster fix his wagon wheel two days ago. He was mighty pleased. They was from Missouri and real tired from the crossing. It might be a good luck piece." Having said that, Senner headed for the Faro table.

By midnight Luke and Senner exited the bar. There was a chill in the air, Luke pulled his poncho tight to his throat. The street was noisy with drunks and wild cowboys coming in and out of the bars whose pianos could be heard mingling with each other and the gun shots fired with exuberance.

"Five hundred bucks! How the hell did you get so lucky? I wouldn't of believed it ifn' I hadn't seed' it myself. Well, what are you goin' to do with all that money?"

Senner grinned lazily. He felt like shouting at the passing riders; instead he headed silently toward the livery with Luke in tow, chattering as they moved. He needed a mule, feed and prospecting equipment. It was just a good thing that the general store was open late on Saturday night because by morning he'd be on his way.

Senner would miss Luke. They had become good friends in the three years of punching cows together. Luke looked real sad when Senner rode off even though Al promised to come and see him when he'd struck paydirt. Luke's forlorn face told him that would probably never happen.

* * *

For several weeks Senner moved from place to place. He knew that it was going to be hard but was frankly surprised at how hard it was. He hadn't given the search all that much thought. Finding the right signs of ore would take talent and experience; he had neither.

Around dusk in the third week he made camp in a dusty wash. The ground was full of soft sand which would make a good bed. There was plenty of wood scattered about and a small stream where he could water the stock and clean up. Sliding from the saddle, the cowboy busied himself untieing the mule's tarp. The animal honked approval. After having its burden removed, the mule moved sideways, stamping and raising billows of dust. Next, a fire was laid inside a circle of rocks. It was cold. The sky off to the west streaked fingers of gold across a fuchsia canvas. It was spectacular enough for the cowboy to mount his horse and ride up onto a sharp rise nearly. This was the time of day he loved best. The winter chill settling onto the desert floor while the sky changed color almost always captivated him and man and beast froze gaping at it. Something caught Al's eye. It was a deer drinking from the stream. Almost without sound Senner drew his rifle from the scabbard, aimed and fired. A satisfied grin followed as he galloped toward the fresh meat. "Tonight, I'll eat hearty," he said into the air. While the mare suckled water noisily, Senner skinned out the catch. Later, stretching his long legs, he inhaled the succulent aroma of slow cooking meat, and drank some of his freshly brewed coffee with a smug smile. True, he hadn't found gold but he was completely satisfied with this life.

The bullet which flew above his head caused him to roll away from the fire instantly. Snatching his rifle with an experienced hand, he returned the shot.

"Hold it, partner," a deep voice yelled. "We was just trying to get your attention! Can we come in? My partner and me ain't had no fresh meat in a while. It sure smells appetisin'."

Senner stood, still clutching the weapon which he used with aplomb. He heaved a sigh, slid the weathered Stetson back onto his head with the barrel tip, and nodded slowly, all the while keeping a finger on the trigger of his rifle. The pair coming down the rise were two old sourdoughs who hadn't had a bath in a spell. And, from the looks of them, the scruffs were probably harmless. Senner relaxed some and led them towards his camp.

Experience qualified cowhands to know cattle and horses; Al knew practically nothing about people except when he didn't like them. This pair was acceptable, he guessed. They ate hearty. . . just about devouring the meat. Al poured them some coffee and offered more beans; then, leaned back on his saddle and listed to them jaw.

Jake, the older of the two, had a deep, raspy voice. We've been prospectin' for gold, Al. But, so far we ain't seen none. Charlie's found some promisin' quartz but not enough to set us to diggin'. What are you doin' in these parts?"

"Same as you, I reckon'."

Charlie got up to get more beans. He seemed half starved. Al had never seen two men eat so much at one time and it occurred to him that maybe they were down on their luck.

"Where'd you learn about ore? I mean you both seem to have some experience."

"Oh, Jake and me come from up Utah way, we prospected Colorado some. We didn't find color but we learned the game. I figure this is a good area. An old guy named Morse filed a claim in here in the early 80's. He was broke and couldn't do his assessment, he abandoned the idea but I hear'd that Kimball, who owns the hotel in Mesa City, has been rootin' around. He's a pretty good businessman. Charlie and me figure if'n he's around there must be sumpin' here?" Charlie nodded his acceptance of the idea. "Well, what about you, Al? Are you prospectin'?"

Senner nodded. "I don't know much about it. I just decided to take a vacation from cows."

"Why don't you put in with us? Charlie and me could always use some help and you seem to be pretty good with that rifle, Al, that's better than anything around here. Them injuns' is fierce. What you say?"

Al told them he'd sleep on it and they could come into camp at breakfast. He'd give them an answer then.

A blaze of stars overhead were ice white on velvet. Senner laid back on his saddle gazing up at them and wondering if Katie had seen them. The night seemed especially glorious. He wondered if his luck was holding bringing the two sourdoughs into his camp. It had to be luck. He accepted that fact, grinning softly he pulled his saddle blanket over his body, and fell into a deep, innocent sleep.

After breakfast the trio headed toward the main Superstition Mountain up a sliced wash. There was enough water in the creek to cause the steady clop of shoes as the animals sloshed along. The musical sound raised around their ears and reminded Al Senner of the Spring roundup when he and Luke worked as a team. It was the first time Senner remembered the boy. That fact startled him. 'A person ought not to forget a friend that easy', he thought. Luke's smiling face appeared in his mind.

Luke reminded Senner a lot of himself when he was that age. Now, at thirty-four the lean cowboy looked used. It was the weather, being out in it day and night. His skin appeared bronze against the shock of unruly, sandy hair which was never combed because he rarely took off his felt. Once anyone actually saw Al Senner's eyes they never forgot them because they were as blue as cornflowers only clear and bright. Even Katie remarked how special they were and Al blushed remembering that. He remembered something else as another face crept into his mind's eye. The man was his mother's brother. A great brute of a human who saw young Al as slave labor after his mother's death. The cowboy winced visualizing the beating he'd been given for some small infraction like not replacing the hay fork in the barn; or, leaving the lead on the plow horse; or coming in from town half-an-hour late because he'd stopped to talk to someone. Senner hated that man. Actually, Benjamin Torence was the reason Al Senner became a cowboy. He recollected that at 16 the skinny, too tall boy just couldn't do anything else. He was 17 when he arrived in the territory; it was 1877. Now, it seemed such a long time ago when he ran away from West Virginia and made his way west hoping to work on a ranch. Then, as luck would have it, he met a miner who offered him a spot at the Silver King. He had been excited to go work in a silver mine where the pay was better, but after a couple of years they closed the mine for repairs and to open new tunnels. Al went back to the ranch to help McKenny with the spring roundup. And, here he was following these two sourdoughs in the hopes of striking paydirt. His thoughts jogged as Charlie called to him to stay closer. He was bored. The ride through washes seemed unending. It went on that way for almost two weeks. On the third week they came into an arroyo and Al took up the rear position. Eventually, Jake raised a hand and hurried to a bank nearby. Al heard him yelling for Charlie to come and look. Al slid from his saddle. He approached to see first hand what these two were hollering about.

"It's quartz, Al, look here." Al leaned into the bank, squinting to see the white rock being exposed by Charlie's eager shovel. He could barely see the gold and the two men were getting excited. He didn't want to seem stupid but he couldn't imagine what all the fuss was about. Charlie ran for pick from his pack mule. Soon he was hacking away at the strata, repeating it until a pile of rock lay at their feet. They sat down to examine it.

"Make camp, Al," Charlie demanded. "I think we've found a good spot."

The excitement was contagious—Senner grinned from ear to ear.

They'd stayed in the washes to remain as inconspicuous as possible. There was no denying it, the Apaches were still a problem and even though the trio were not actually inside the range, their proximity could be dangerous. One thing was encouraging, the savages usually didn't move at night; so, their fire probably wouldn't be seen.

Al busied himself setting up the camp. From above no one could see that they were in the area. It would be dark within a couple of hours. He scanned the sky casually and frowned deeply at the sight of heavy, dark clouds forming to the west. His partners were anxiously hacking at the quartz and the sound of the pick chopping the rock was reassuring. He moved closer to the activity and heard Charlie's mounting enthusiasm. "Jake, look at this stuff, hot damn." He lifted it to the sky dancing around in the sand.

For the first time Senner spoke. "Are you guys sure this is

the real thing?"

"Sure! Sure! Ha! Ha! Al, we got a winner. I'm tellin' you this is it!"

Al strained to look at Jake's bearded face. The look was solid joy. It was not until then he actually believed he might have Katie. Suddenly, they were all dancing in the wash, yelling and throwing the rock at each other. Al raced back to the mule where he produced the bottle of whiskey he'd been carrying for medicinal purposes. He threw it to Jake who took a big swig and threw it to Charlie. As it happened they finished it off, burping happily and swaying in the twilight. They were all drunk. Finally, Charlie fell down. The other two collapsed—laughing and yelling and rolling on the earth. Jake said they had to go into town to file the claim but somebody had to stay with the strike. It didn't take long to convince the cowboy because he was the best shot, he should be the protector. Al capitulated before falling sound asleep.

Chapter 2

A Stolen Dream

It was well before sun-up when the storm broke. A crash of thunder overhead startled the cowboy who sat up, grabbed a rifle and jumped quickly to his feet. Above, a searing lightning bolt exposed a leaden sky. He glared at it, disbelieving the enormity of the storm. His head was splitting and the noise only increased his pain. Shortly, a torrent of rain pelted Al's weary body and knowing the drill he was sure that trying to hurry wouldn't work; he was still drunk and motion seemed extra hard. Lightning flashed. The valley was illuminated again and again, exposing the main mountain and the fury being unleashed upon the entire area. It occurred to him that he didn't see anyone else. Shouting for Charlie over the din seemed useless. Al hurried as best he could, throwing a saddle over the mare and grabbing at the mule's lead. He thought it a blessing that she still had some of her pack on. He tossed the saddle blanket atop the saddle and pulled the fish from under the cantle. The rain was blinding now. The fish would help some; every cowboy had one. There was no time to look for the gear. His boot hit the coffee pot, bending; Al snatched it before swinging into the saddle and quickly dug a rowel into the mare. They literally raced up the wash toward the main mountain where a huge overhang gaped at them. The animal's eyes mirrored her terror; Senner knew she hated storms. Within twenty minutes they moved inside the cave-like rock formation; then, for a long time, horse, mule and cowboy just sat motionless, thankful for the sheer rock haven curving out, high above their heads. Senner climbed down. He patted the horse lovingly and spoke into her ear. "Good old girl. You did it again. Thanks, Lady. It won't be long before a raging wall of water will be roaring through that arroyo. You just saved my life. . .again." He grinned knowingly and mumbled, "You don't like these storms anymore than I do. . .I sure know that."

They were higher now. Each flash lit the valley just slightly below them preceding repeated thunder claps. It was a furious storm and All knew what danger could lurk in the washes and arroyos. Every cowboy feared the storms which came on so suddenly, high up, dumping gallons of water into the bone dry washes which would fill and build until a wall of water would roll down the canyons and ride over a camp like a train. He'd lost some friends in two of them and had seen cattle drowned quickly because they were unable to get out of the way in time. For a long moment he relived the accident involving the ranch owner's son, Jeff. They were following the herd for roundup. It was nearly dark when the storm came on. The boy had been told so many times to stay out of the washes when a bad storm came on suddenly, but he seemed unable to understand fear. Al remembered with a shudder seeing the young man ride up the arroyo after a calf. They were all yelling to him. He ignored their cries. Seconds later the water surged through the valley and swallowed him up right in front of their horror struck stares. They didn't find his body for a week and the old man was never the same after the loss.

The suddenness of his movements and the fresh air sobered Senner who was slowly remembering all the previous night's festivities. Charlie and Jake had cut out. He frowned deeply while moving about the cave trying to find something with which to start a fire. He came upon a few pieces of dried cow manure and some drift left over from a previous camp. It made the task easier. Soon there was light and warmth available. Lady moved closer to him and nickered softly; they would both enjoy the fire. Al lifted the saddle and put it aside before trying to dry her with the saddle blanket, talking softly and stroking the animal with a tender hand. Besides Katie, Lady was the only being he had ever loved. The big mare's eyes reflected appreciation. Later, he took care of the mule and the animals huddled close together for warmth. "Good thing I grabbed this pot," he said out loud, "I hate being without my coffee when it's wet." The animals watched with interest as he performed the task while the aroma from the fresh brew filled their nostrils and billowing smoke rose inside the walls. In time it was cosy. Al heard the roar and hurried to the ledge outside his camp. Patiently, he waited for a flash bright enough to expose the arroyo, and then he saw it. A tidal wave of water and rock and trees sucked along as the flash flood picked up momentum and raced through the canyons of the Superstitions and out into the valley, washing away the place where he had slept and where he would still be if he hadn't awakened.

Resting on the saddle, sipping the fresh coffee and trying to dry out, gave the cowboy time to reflect on the matters at hand. 'They must have come to, seen the storm coming and just packed up. Seems like they might of roused me first.' The puzzle kept him up for a couple of hours while the storm continued. Much later, he slept, but it was fitful.

By late morning Senner was dry and rested. He collected some feed for the animals and while they ate he climbed up on a ledge, trying to see where their camp had been. From his vantage point he could see down the arroyo for a half mile. 'It couldn't have been much further than that.' Naturally, there wouldn't be anything left after the storm, he knew that—but, he might be able to find the spot where they camped—if he took it slow and examined the walls of the cut. He saddled the mare and left the mule hobbled. She had food and had been watered. He'd come for her later.

Lady stepped into the wet sand carefully. A lot of rock had come down out of the range with the flood and the washes were still running full. Al was careful to observe the signs of the ride he had taken as best as he could remember in a drunken condition. One of the things a cowboy learned early on was to make a mental note each time he saw an unusual rock formation, tree, fence or cut in a mountain. Something to mark a place so, if he needed to return at least he would be able to find it. This wasn't going to be easy. It had been dark and stormy and he'd had a belly full of rot gut whiskey to boot. Senner sneered. They moved really slow on the high side of the wash. The big arroyo was in front of them and Senner saw a crooked palo verde hanging over a ledge in some tall rocks about a mile down. It nudged his memory. "Hot doggie!" he yelled, "Git along, Lady, I know that tree." Once they reached the tree, he realized that everything had changed in the area. The raging water had torn away a huge piece of the wall of the arroyo. It was hard to imagine where the camp was. Every bit of equipment had been carried away; boulders on the banks were toppled into each other; wet sand piled high had mounded near a bend and it seemed almost like a new place. Senner leaned on the saddle horn.

Shaking his head he said, "Lady, I don't know where we was?"

Almost instantly the sun came from behind a cloud. Senner lifted his shoulders enjoying the warmth of the rays on his neck and back. He sighed. "That's a good feel, Lady. Ain't nothin' like it to warm a man's bones." With that statement, Al pulled off the felt and lifted his face to the sun—smiling wide. The horse stamped and snorted approval. She too was enjoying the warmth on her damp coat. After looking at the sun Senner squinted badly. Something off to the left was dazzling. He rubbed his eyes and looked again. Sunlight dancing on the wall of the arroyo had settled on an exposed vein of gold. Its dull brilliance startled the cowboy but even Al knew what it had to be. Leaping off the mare and racing towards it, the cowboy shouted and twisted, jumping up and throwing his hat into the air.

"Yahoooo......Katie, I found gold.....Ya Hoooooooooo." ......Even Lady responded.

For the next four days Al Senner and Lady searched the path of the flood. So far, he'd found a pick ax, two pots and a canteen; all very much needed items. He made a new camp. The mule still had oats, coffee and some flour in her tarp. He shot a couple of rabbits, skinned them out, ate the meat and made pouches out of the skins.

The weather turned sunny and warm. It took almost a week before the caliche dried out and eventually, he could make a dry bed on soft sand.

During the day, Al sought out all of the trees and wood debris which tumbled out of the washes, collecting in a tangled web of rocks. He laid it out to dry and soon there was plenty of firewood. In between time he used the pick-ax to chop off the gold from the big vein exposed by the flood waters. The gold was so rich sometimes he could barely extract it because of the wire gold holding it. The rabbits' fur made excellent pouches. Al carefully cleaned the quartz away from the ore, washed it in the stream and put it into the skins. When time allowed he took it back to the big overhang, found a deep crevice near the back and cached the gold ore. At least he had a head start on claiming his lady love. He reckoned that when the prospectors returned the work would begin in earnest.

Early in the morning of the second week, he awakened to the sound of horses and wagons moving towards the mountains. Climbing up, Al saw the billows of dust preceding a caravan. There were a lot of riders.

His camp had been moved to the overhang since it had turned cold and most of the firewood was stored there to keep it dry in case of storm. The tall cowboy stretched and yawned before saying, "Well, I'll be damned!" Down below, coming up the wash was what looked to be a wagon train. Al saddled Lady even before he had his coffee. As he rode towards the on-coming wagons, he saw four men in a carriage. Approaching them,

Al pulled off his hat and called, "Hello, riders." Before they answered he recognized one of them; it was Charlie. But, not the Charlie he'd known, instead this man was shaved and bathed; wearing a pin striped suit and bowler hat. Al jerked on the mare's rein, gaping wide mouthed. "CHARLIE! Is that you?"

Charlie's face turned down, a scowl formed and he looked away.

Glancing from one to the other, Al saw Jake in similar garb. "Well, I'll be." He said it with absolute amazement. Neither man spoke to him.

One of the other riders said, "What do you want, Sir?"

Senner blanched. "What I want is my share of the mine . . . Damn sure, that's what I want."

The man had spoken with authority. He waved to two riders who immediately surrounded Senner and knocked him off his horse with a rifle butt. Hurt and shocked, Senner lay glaring up at the four of them and rubbing at his sore shoulder.

One of the strangers said, "I am Denny Sullivan, Mr. Hall and I own this claim. I suggest you get on your horse and get out of here, now."

Jake rasped out. "Now wait a minute, Mr. Sullivan. This fellow used to work for us. He's good with a gun—why not put him on? Those Apaches are still raising hell out here. It wouldn't hurt none."

Senner got up. A rage was building subverted beneath his silence. Knowing he couldn't stand off so many, his mind raced over the offer; then he acquiesced without so much as a word. Mounting Lady, the cowboy rode off toward the overhang without looking back.

At that moment one of them spotted the exposed vein and pandemonium broke out. For the rest of the night Senner sat in his hide-out listening to the sounds of a camp being set up. Anger mounted inside of him and he paced. Anger wasn't his style; he never thought of revenge before, even when his uncle stole his mother's farm, but this? Down below was Katie and

Superstitions Become Realities.

C. L. Hall, of Leadville, Colorado, has bonded from Orlando and O. D Merrill, J. R. Morse and C. B. Hakes, the Black Queen, Black Hawk, Mother Hubbard, Tom Thumb and Mammoth, good mining claims, in the Superstition mountains, for $20,000, payable on or before July 3, 1893. Mr. Hall is an old miner, accustomed to handling big properties. His interest in these claims shows that the Superstition mining country is liable to come speedily to the front.

Clip from Arizona Gazette, *1893.*

the future he had planned to build with her. "Damn them... Damn them...." he shouted it over and over. There wasn't any sleep that night and by morning he'd made a decision. He built a good fire then dropped the left over rabbit into it. The coffee smelled strong brewing. After he ate Al packed up the mule with extreme care, putting the sacks of gold in between his stores. Finally, he mounted Lady and rode slowly toward the tent city already teaming with toughs, miners, cowboys and a few dance hall girls straggling in early for their share of the promised riches.

The place was alive with activity. Senner found the best looking tent on a bluff above the town. That one would belong to the owner. He approached astride the mare, calling to Hall in a firm voice. The owner appeared without his coat and holding a shaving mug full of foam and a brush. He stared up soberly.

"I've decided to take a job here, Mr. Hall," Senner said, "but I want to be a foreman in the mine. I'll ride shotgun, if trouble comes, but just now I need to make some money."

Hall appeared to be thinking it over. "Alright, you are hired. Go tell the manager, he's in the big tent in the center down there. You'll get $50.00 per month and that's top dollar. And, Mr.,

I want no more trouble. . .do you hear me?" Senner nodded. "I'll be goin' into Mesa City for supplies. Be back in three days."

Hall started into the tent, then reconsidering he paused and said, "Senner, sometimes people lose. I'm sorry. I will see to it that you come out alright." Then, turning, he walked through the flaps.

* * *

It was a five hour horse ride to Mesa City. Al knew Katie would be wondering where he'd gone, and, since everybody would be talking about the new gold strike he imagined she would think that's where he'd be. A smile erupted. Just thinking about his girl made him happy. It was a wondrous thing.

By noon Al rode into town; by three P.M. he'd had a bath, a shave and a haircut and at five sharp he'd appeared at the Kimball House Hotel in new clothes, smelling special and headed for Katie's corner table. His heart leaped when he saw her. She was wearing that pale blue dress she'd made and a white apron with hand crocheted lace which went all the way to the floor. The long red locks were done up in a top knot but a few strands hung wispy around her green eyes. It embarrassed him to look at her because he knew he must be beet red.

Katie had been down on the dining room floor only a short time. She worked breakfast and dinner hours in the big pleasant room and agreed it was not the best job in the world but it would do. The miners tipped good when things went well and the townsfolk were mighty nice to her. Except for the drunks, who were ugly, life was fairly pleasant. She still waited for that Al Senner to come back. He was handsome and bronzed and had the bluest eyes she had ever seen. Of course, he promised her the moon and a whole lot more, which was what they all said, but, he was still her favorite.

The dining room filled quickly for supper. Most of the tables were full now except for the one in the corner. Katie stopped.

She saw him there and her heart fluttered; she smiled sweetly. Al stood to greet her.

"Evenin' Miss Katie."

"Evenin', Al. My, you look nice and you smell nice too." She laughed.

Her laughter always reminded Al of the glass chimes in the Chinamen's laundry which tinkled when the wind blew.

"It is good to hear your laugh, Katie." He flushed slightly, feeling awkward.

"Why don't you sit down and I'll get you some coffee while you decide. I have to work until eight o'clock, so, if you care to, we can talk then."

Al nodded. He ate the meal she brought. There were extra rolls and thick cream butter and homemade jam accompanying the stew. Two pieces of pie were served afterwards with plenty of black coffee. Al never remembered being so full, but it was all done with a loving hand. After supper he told Katie he would spend time in the town and come back for her later.

The assay office would be open. Al crossed the street and stepped up onto the boardwalk, walking briskly towards it. Clutching his poncho tight, the cowboy ignored the night air by concentrating on the parade of horse riders and cowboys in from the spreads with money in their pockets cluttering the dusty street. It seemed strange to him to be hearing the street noises and people talking. Somehow it made him believe, even momentarily, that he belonged, and he liked it.

Once inside the shop, while the clerk helped another customer, Al waited, passing the time examining ore samples until he heard the other customer leave and a voice say, "Can I help you?"

"Yea. I've brought some ore in. I'd like it assayed and I'd like to sell some." Al pulled out two sacks made from rabbit skin, untied them and dumped the contents onto the wood counter.

The assayer whistled. "That's rich stuff. Where'd you get this?"

"Out north east of here."

"I've seen this ore before. . .yea, just this week. Them two prospectors filed a claim on that property. . .It's called the Mammoth Mine #1. You must have hear'd about it? Why, they sold their claim to two rich fellers from Denver for $20,000.00. Can you imagine that? What luck."

Senner tried to appear nonchalant—his blood started to boil while the color deepened on his face and beneath the counter his fists clenched although he remained silent.

"Did you know them?" the assayer asked.

"Yea." Al inhaled sharply. "They was a slick as calves' slobbers."

The man looked up over his spectacles. He had heard that remark before and judging from the cowboy's grimace, decided to drop the subject.

It was silent while the assayer weighed out the gold. "Well, gold is paying $20.20 per ounce and you've got quite a bit here." He stood figuring with a pencil then looked up and smiled. "Yes, sir, just as I thought—it comes to well over $700.00 worth. That's okay, wouldn't you say?"

Al nodded and looked expectant.

The assayer turned and went to the safe.

After he was paid, Al tipped his hat and left. He clomped down the boardwalk towards the merchantile. It was warm inside and several people were gathered around the pot-bellied stove talking about the big strike near the Goldfield Mountains. Al stopped to put some gum drops into a paper sack from the candy barrel and then, went to the counter to await his turn.

"Can I help you, Mister?"

"Oh, yea. I was wonderin' ifn' you had a necklace—you know, a gold one?"

The clerk was obviously not young, he smiled. "Sure, come over here. Got some nice gold hearts. They is new and the ladies like 'em real much." He walked to the far end of the counter and leaned down extracting a tray of jewelry which he put in front of the cowboy with a flourish. He seemed quite proud of the merchandise.

Al examined them carefully. "How much?"

"Well, this engraved one come all the way from St. Louis. It's a real beauty—don't you think?" He held it in the lamp light, it glistened and swung in a circle.

"How much?" Al seemed impatient but it was obvious he liked the piece.

"It is $30.00, but it's real gold. Oh, and it come from one of those rich jewelry stores. It even has a black velvet ribbon to wear it on."

"I'll take it. Wrap it nice, my girl likes nice things."

The clerk moved away toward the wrapping paper, grinning softly to himself. Once the package was put together he handed it to the cowboy in exchange for three ten dollar gold pieces. He stood watching the big man exit and thought how lucky his lady was.

* * *

John Ravick

Filed and recorded at request of M. B. Fleishman Jan-12-1893 at 2 P.M.

Neri Osborn
County Recorder

Location Notice

Notice is hereby given that we the undersigned having complied with the requirements of Chapter 6 of title thirty two of the revised statutes of the United States and the local customs, laws and regulations, have located 1500 feet in length by 600 feet in width on this lode or vein of Mineral bearing quartz. The boundaries of this mine are as follows, commencing at this monument and running 300 feet southerly thence 1500 feet westerly thence 600 feet northerly thence 1500 feet easterly thence 300 feet southerly to place of beginning. This mine is situated on the south side of the Vulture Hala mountains and is the first west extension of the Lucky Cuss mine Maricopa County Arizona Territory and shall be known as the Silver Crown

Dated January 1st 1893

Locators
M. S. Moffott
Carmelita Campbell
John Ravick

Filed and recorded at request of M. B. Fleishman Jan. 12- 1893 at 2 P.M.

Neri Osborn
County Recorder

Notice of Location. Book 5 page 461-462

Of the mammoth Mining claim on the Mammoth quartz ledge containing gold and silver and located as a gold and silver quartz mine the undersigned claim for Mining purposes. Fifteen Hundred (1500) feet of this quartz ledge in length along the ledge or vein and Three hundred (300) feet on each side of the middle of the vein at the surface. Together with all dips spurs and angles and all valuable mineral deposits contained therein and all timber growing within the limits of said claim and all water and water privileges thereon or appurtenant thereto under and according to the provisions of an act of Congress approved May 10 1872 entitled an act to promote the development of the mining resources of the United States" and all acts amendatory thereto, and the laws of the Territory of Arizona. This claim commences at this notice which is posted in a monument of stone in a conspicuous place on the ledge at the north center end boundary of the claim and running thence three hundred (300) feet in a westerly direction to a monument of stone and a stake marked north west corner; thence fifteen hundred (1500) feet in a southerly direction to a monument of stone and a stake marked south west corner; thence three hundred (300) feet in an easterly direction to a monument of stone and a stake marked south center monument and boundary; thence three hundred (300) feet in an easterly direction to a monument of stone and a stake marked south east corner; thence fifteen hundred (1500) feet in a northerly direction to a monument of stone and a stake marked north east corner thence three hundred (300) feet in a westerly direction to the place of beginning. This claim may be more generally described as situated in Superstition mountain in Maricopa County Arizona Territory and joining the Tom Thumb mining claim on the south and shall be known as the Mammoth claim and the - - - .

dated on the ground this 26th day of November A.D. 1892

— Company Witnesses — | Signed Orlando Merrill
J. R. Morse
D. L. Merrill
C. R. Hakes

Filed for record at the request of C. R. Hakes January 12th A.D. 1893 at 15 min. past 10 A.M.

[illegible] County Recorder

Notice of Location

Of the Black King Mining claim on the - - - quartz ledge Containing - - - - and located as a gold and silver quartz mine the undersigned claim for mining purposes Fifteen Hundred (1500) feet of this quartz ledge in length along the ledge or vein and three hundred 300) feet on each side

Claim on Mammoth, Recorded January 12, 1893.

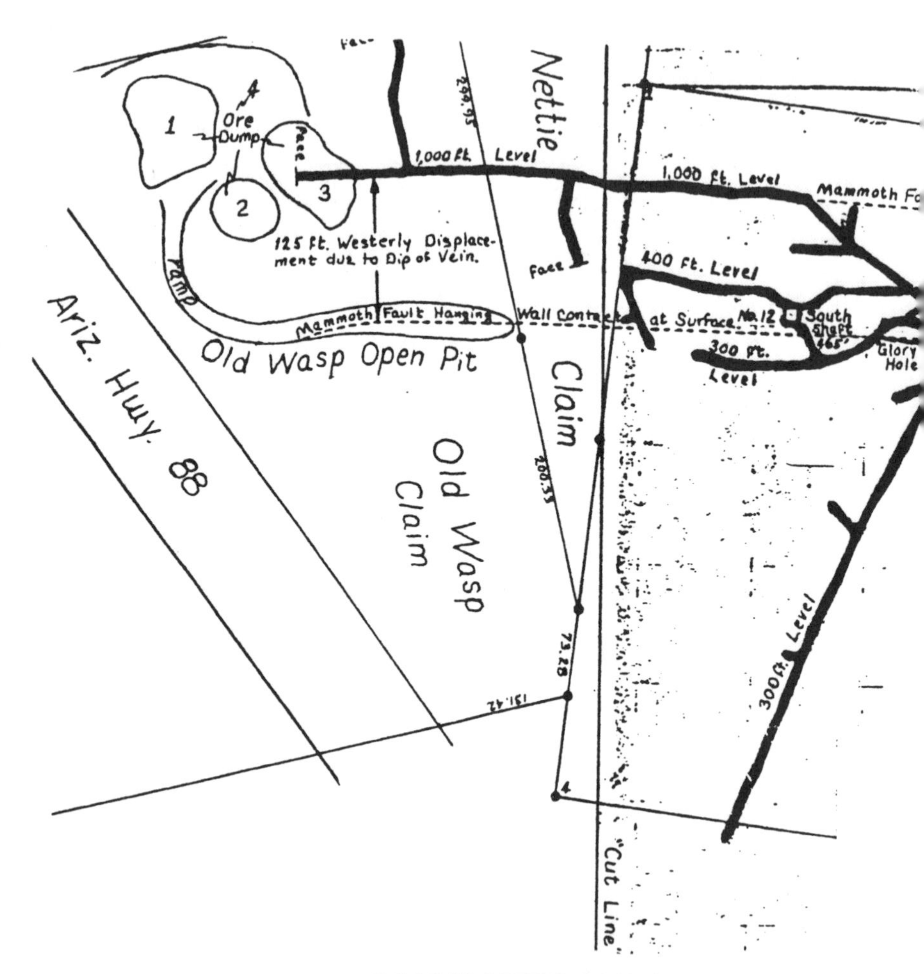

MAMMOTH MINE

Levels A through 800 ft. mapped 4-17-1923 by E.W. Bedford(?). 1,000 ft, level added from survey (Overpeck & Hardinger) 11-03-1925. Shaft locations & culture from M.S.3886. Only available copy was black & white (color coding lost). Portion south of "Cut Line" added and all levels identified and recoded 10-15-1988 by Clay Worst from plats by Bedford & Hardinger. All levels shown as of 11-03-1925.

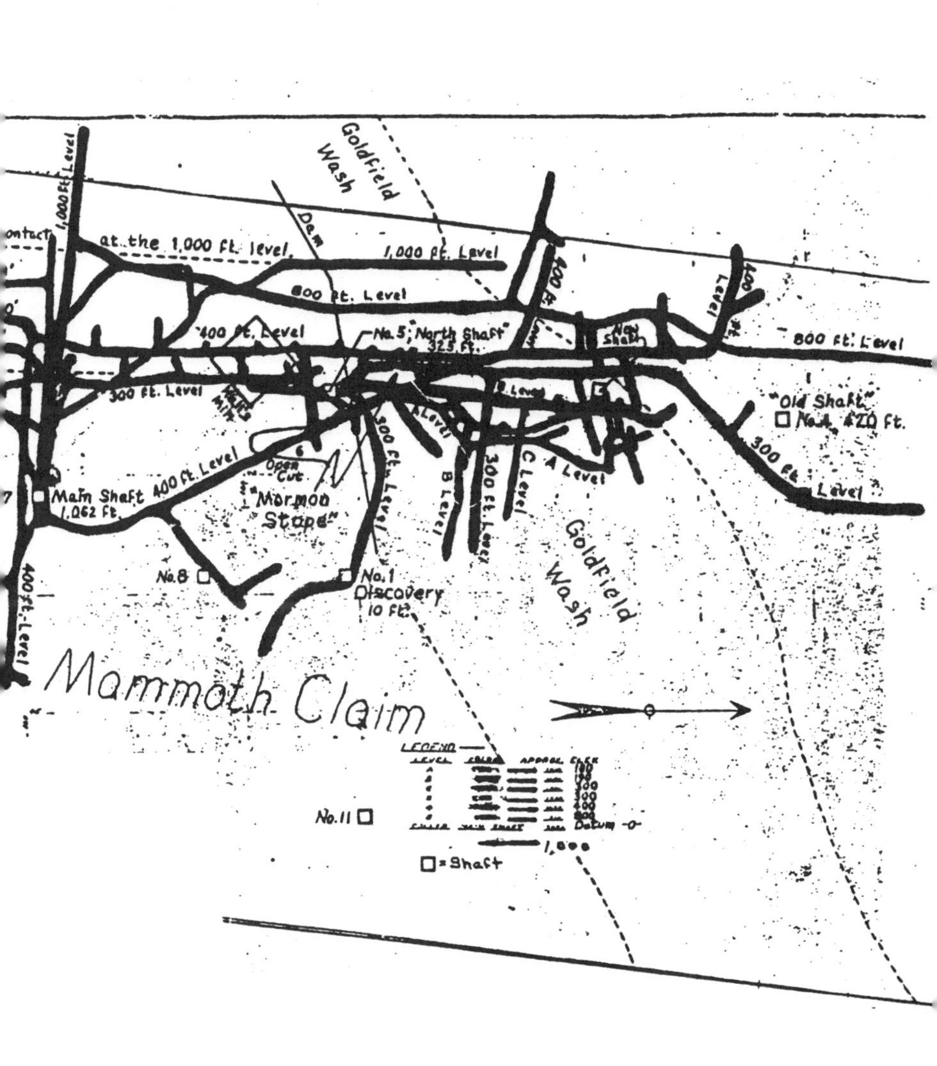
Goldfield Wash
1,000 ft. Level
at the 1,000 ft. level
Dam
1,000 ft. Level
800 ft. Level
400 ft. Level
No. 5 "North Shaft" 325 ft.
400 ft.
New Shaft
400 ft. Level
800 ft. Level
300 ft. Level
"Old Shaft" No. 4 420 ft.
300 ft. Level
Open Cut
"Mormon Stope"
Main Shaft 1,062 ft.
400 ft. Level
300 ft. Level
B Level
300 ft. Level
C Level
A Level
Goldfield Wash
No. 8
No. 1 Discovery 10 ft.
400 ft. Level
Mammoth Claim
Legend
Datum -0-
1,000
No. 11
= Shaft

Chapter 3

Katie

At eight o'clock sharp Katie exited the dining room. Excited, hurrying up the curving kitchen staircase, she rushed over worn carpets to the corner room where she lived. Once inside she filled the chipped crock basin with water and began to wash. The lovely face staring out of the mirror looked flushed and exuberant as she brushed her long auburn hair before smoothing it and tying on a green satin ribbon. A smug smile arose. In the cupboard was a new dress made especially for this occasion out of a bolt of green taffeta ordered from Denver which cost two weeks' wages, and which was sewn with care and joy as she imagined this particular night. The frock rustled as Katie pulled it on. The slowest part was buttoning a long row of tiny buttons up the bodice front. Katie giggled, twisting and turning in front of the mirror. The wool cape, which hung over the cupboard door, wasn't good enough for this occasion. She sighed, frowning, 'It would have to do.' Her love of fine things was evident from the look of delight reflected in her sparkling eyes. Deep down, Katie believed that in due time all of her wishes would come true.

The Pioneer House, Mr. Kimball's new hotel, was the pride of Mesa City. He was especially proud of its curving, oak staircase recently imported from Denver, and which also served the old structure where Katie and the other workers lived.

Katie hurried towards it knowing Al would be down in the lobby. At the head of the stairs she smoothed the taffeta, put the cape inconspicuously over the other arm, lifted the long skirt daintily, raised her head to an elegant position and started down. The lobby was full of guests. None of them missed the entrance, especially Al Senner patiently leaning against a wooden pillar just outside of the dining room. The satisfaction growing on his face became more evident as he straightened to full height and started eagerly towards the bottom of the steps.

Approaching, ten gallon in hand, Al said, "Evenin' Miss Katie. You look especially fine tonight."

"Hello, Al." Her smile told him all he needed to know.

He offered his arm awkwardly. The momentary embarrassment stemmed from the attention Katie was receiving from every other person in the room.

"I rented a buggy," he said softly, before replacing his Stetson and leading the young woman out onto the boardwalk.

Shortly, the pair climbed into the waiting carriage. It was cold but not unpleasant; Katie leaned against her man for warmth. Al sat straight, clucking at the horse which pranced down Main Street. They drove in silence for about twenty minutes until the buggy started up a slight rise. Al reined it up after turning it onto a flat open area where they could see the lights of the town.

"Whoa there, boy." Pulling up on the reins, the cowboy tied them off before turning to Katie.

"I guess you've been a wonderin' where I've been?"

Katie nodded.

"I've been trying to find a way to get a stake." He glanced away. "I mean I know you deserve a good life and I mean to give it to you."

"I know you will try, Al. I honestly do."

"Look! Katie, look here." He pulled out the box purchased at the mercantile and put it into her hands.

"What's this?" She was genuinely surprised. Her hand shook a little as she opened it. "Oh, Al, it is beautiful." Her face lit and the green eyes danced with sheer pleasure. "Put it on me, quick."

Al took the ribbon in his big hands while Katie lifted her long hair and turned away so he could fasten it around her neck.

"There!" he said, grinning. "It's on and it looks real nice."

Katie threw her hands around his neck impulsively. "Oh, Al, I love it but it looks so expensive. Are you sure you can afford this? I mean I didn't want you to spend your last dime on a present."

He laughed. "No. I didn't, I could afford it. I got a real job out in Goldfield as a foreman in the mine. I aim to get us a stake so we can get married, like you said." He became serious, looking right into her eyes. "See Katie, I ain't never loved nobody before. I'm not sure what to do but I got an ache for you that's somethin' awful."

He grabbed her and kissed her hard. Katie gasped when he let her go.

"I love you too, Al."

"You do? Damn, that sounds swell. Say it again."

He held her a long time after that and she said many things to him including "I love you," over and over. He never tired of hearing her say it. He wanted to tell her how he lost the mine but a man couldn't do that. It was his place to get her what she wanted and needed, no matter what he had to do. In that moment, in that quiet place with the stars for witnesses, Al Senner made his resolve. He would give her everything there was—a fine house, jewelry, beautiful clothes, befittin' such a lady, and all the things that went with it. He was almost impatient to get started. But for now, on this particular night, he wanted just to be with his lady love.

* * *

They went on a picnic the following day. Mr. Kimball was good about letting the help trade days off. Katie couldn't believe

Goldfield, Arizona 1893 *Credit: Salt River Project History Services*

her joy. She wore the golden heart from that day on and everyone remarked how pretty it was. Late that night, after supper and time together, they said goodby. Al couldn't remember anything being that hard. They would be apart for a long time and he wanted to remember every word and detail while he effected his revenge.

The ride back to Goldfield took five hours. Al loped along on Lady. It was almost midnight by the time he arrived at the overhang. He guessed he'd try to build a shack down the wash, but it would have to be away from all of that commotion.

By now, the place was swarming with people. Wagons came in daily with supplies for the ever-growing town and the mine, which was rumored to be the richest lode in the West. Of course, there were other claims being worked nearby and they were drawing people in from all over. Gunslingers arrived to ride shotgun with the ore. Transients, just after what ever they could steal or grab off the workers, slipped in daily hoping for a quick dollar. Stage coaches arrived bearing painted ladies and their maids ready to work in the newly built saloons. There were piano players, bartenders, waitresses, cooks, hotel and tradespeople all milling about the not quite built town. Some slept in their wagons but most of them lived in tents with hastily built palm frond porches. Fortunately, Goldfield had plenty of water. In fact, the mines were already having a problem in the lower levels filling with seepage. Pumps had to be put into operation. The water eventually became a pond. Unseasoned new comers often became ill drinking the overflow which was rich in minerals.

At sunup Al fixed coffee and fed the stock. While they watered, he climbed up onto the ledge to see what was taking place down below. The sound of picks and sledges hitting rock echoed loud. There was hammering from carpenters building a restaurant and a hotel and there was even going to be a mercantile which had its early stock piled up in a big canvas overhang. The tents for the gaming places were already in full swing and a cook was clanging away at a triangle outside of

Drillers working underground.
Photo courtesy of Arizona Historical Society Library.

one of them.

Of course, the mine would run three shifts. Al saddled Lady and rode towards the newly formed tunnel expecting to check in with Traymore Gillford, the mine manager, first.

The office tent was full when he rode in. He could hear loud voices and people shifting in and out as he tied up the mare. Al awaited his turn. The man in front of him was a powerful looking black man. He smiled to Senner as they moved toward the tent's flap, saying, "This part is always unpleasant, isn't it?"

Senner grinned lazily. "You experienced in mines?"

The black man threw his head back and laughed. "No, Sir. But I intend to be, for sure."

Before they could continue, he was called inside the tent. The manager smiled broadly when he heard him say he was a shooter.

"We need blasters bad. Good to have you."

The conversation ended and Senner approached the table nodding slightly to the black soldier who passed by on his way out.

Traymore greeted him with a sneer.

"Are you the guy what tried to claim some of Mr. Hall's mine?"

"Look, Mr. Gillford, I had a deal with them two prospectors. How was I supposed to know they'd cut me out?"

The manager leaned across the table right into Senner's face and spat out. "You try any funny business here, Senner. The bulls are here to take care of just that stuff. You got it?"

Senner stared at the man. His eyes appeared stoic, masking the hatred in his heart.

"Did you hear me?"

"Yea. I hear'd you. Now, can we get on with our business?"

By nine-thirty Al Senner was casting men into their positions. The early job at the Silver King was enough to convince them of his experience. True, he lied about being a foreman but he figured the knowledge would come with time. He just had to be good at whatever he did for them. Everyone knew miners were usually tough, dishonest and clever. There were a lot of tricks to the game and he had been young and green when he learned them but he answered their questions satisfactorily.

There were twenty new ones in that day. Al smiled inwardly at the look of them; they were rough-neck, hooligans whose faces were likely hanging on a jail house wall somewhere. Of course, nobody cared, just as long as they could swing a pick and had brawn. Most of them showed up with their resin covered hard hats which could only have been made when they worked in the mines. Their uniforms were short sleeved under-shirts, union drawers under baggy trousers with no visible means of support and ankle high brogans on their feet. Some even carried slick oilskin covers for down in the wet parts of the dig. When it was hot there was condensation and while they sweated they could be cooled quickly during winter months and many of them died of pneumonia. Often they brought sheepskin covers to hang on hooks in the changing rooms.

Of course, occasionally someone showed up in cowboy boots and a ten gallon hat bragging about his experience. Al always sent them to handle the wagons and stock, knowing full well that cowboys didn't know a shovel from a pick.

Being foreman gave Senner a sense of power as he told them they were hired and where he would send them. He was surprised to learn that Trooper was a shooter. They feigned ignorance of each other when they came into contact. It wasn't smart to let toughs know you were friendly with the foreman. The big, black soldier shifted uneasily as Senner directed him toward the tunnel to the left.

"You'd best be gitt'n down there, soldier. They need to blow some quartz and I guess, you are the guy what does it?"

Trooper answered with a grin, "Yes, sir, boss. I'll go now."

Senner watched him disappear into the tunnel. A steady stream of muckers carrying rock out of the tunnel and into the waiting wagons occupied him for the next two hours.

Down in the mine, Trooper moved toward the quartz wall. It was quiet now except for muffled voices fading out of the cave. The holes weren't drilled yet, and the black man lifted a huge hammer and a steel rod with a slightly flaring chisel-bit tip which he placed against a pre-marked spot and connected. Soon the silence was filled with the steady clang of steel on steel. Trooper sweated profusely. The steel rod was turned after each hit. Eventually, he pulled out the rod and shot some water into the hole before pressing a rod in, then withdrawing it. A hard bang was heard as the powerful arm rapped the rod against rock to clean it of wet quartz mud. Trooper repeated the process over and over until the hole was a foot or more deeper. Then he went the next mark and started again. When his laborious work was finished he had a series of holes ready to be plugged. Trooper stood back to admire the job. It was a precision effect. When the holes were shot they primed each other causing concussion. Shooters were specialists and Trooper took pride in his work. "This," he said into the air, "is a specially good job."

Trooper moved about the cave looking for tools left by careless miners. He knew the danger of steel flying around the tunnel after an explosion. Gathering the equipment took only a short while; then, he went up to the next level to pick up his black powder caps. Back down in the chamber, Trooper adjusted his head lamp so it would shine directly in front of him. He carefully placed the pre-prepared caps into the holes and tamped wet clay into them to hold the caps in place. When they were all set it was time to apply the fuses leaving exacting rattails hanging down the face of the collar. Trooper smiled. This moment always gave him a thrill. Yelling, "FIRE IN THE HOLE" he lit the spitter and quickly turned to light each fuse. Within seconds he felt the fire burning his fingers. He dropped the spitter and moved rapidly up the cavern until he came to a huge bend where he slowed to listen for the explosions counting each one to make certain his caps detonated. Satisfaction laced his grin as he entered the lead tunnel and walked out into the sunlight.

Because the job was new, Trooper reflected momentarily on the first experience he'd had when the army was blasting a tunnel in the mountains to be used to store powder, arms and supplies. They were very careful not to explode the whole mountain. The sergeant who taught him was very particular. Trooper remembered grinning. It had been satisfying to have a white man treat him with such respect. He also knew he was the sergeant's prized pupil. Later, when the Indians had been subdued, the instructor taught him all of the tricks. That knowledge probably saved his life a number of times and now, it was providing him with a good job.

At the end of the day, Al climbed the hill to the bar. It was inside a tent. Some rough board tables and benches had been put together. He dropped into one of them and ordered a beer. A black ex-soldier slid in beside of him.

"You want some company?" he said half apologetically.

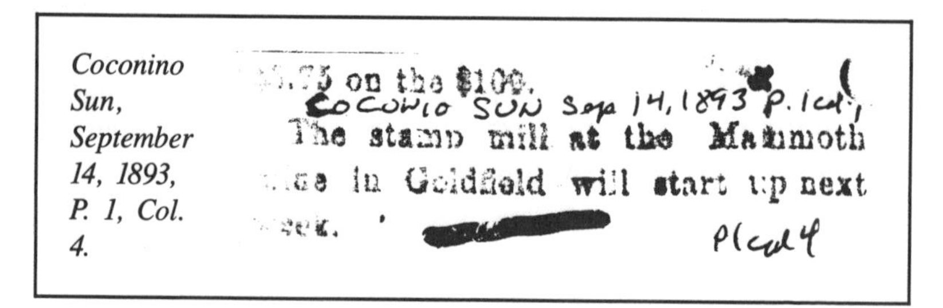
Coconino Sun, September 14, 1893, P. 1, Col. 4.

.75 on the $100.

Coconino Sun Sep 14, 1893 p. 1 col. 1

The stamp mill at the Mammoth ...e in Goldfield will start up next ...ek.

p1 col 4

Senner nodded. "I just ordered a beer. You want one?"

"Yea. I'm powerful thirsty. That dust in the mine clogs your throat."

"You always been in the army?" Al glanced at the cap he was wearing while he signaled the barmaid for two drinks.

"I was soldierin' forever. . . Then, they sent a troop of us out West. I figured I'd try my luck here—got nothin' to go back to."

Senner took the beers. He passed one over and said, "Where did you learn to blast?"

"I learned in the army, fightin' Injuns. It came in handy. By the way, Baker's the name, James Earl my granpappy called me." He exposed a pearly grin, "You can call me Trooper."

"Okay, Trooper." Senner laughed and swallowed the beer quickly. He gave his name and they talked briefly before Senner said, "I'm headed back to my digs. I'll see you tomorrow."

Lady clopped slowly up the wash. The mule heard them coming and honked loudly. Senner clucked to urge Lady on. "Sounds like your friend is hungry, Lady. Come to think of it. . .so am I."

He fed the stock and built a fire. It didn't take long to warm up the leftover deer meat he'd hung in a nearby tree. While the coffee cooked, Al sat down and mused over the day's events.

The mine was in full operation now. It would take a month or so to open up new tunnels, but they were making progress. There were wagons coming in daily with ore cars and equipment to crush and separate. The toughest men were being put down below to break rock and load it. Soon there would be a huge dump near the tunnels and eventually, the rail-cars would empty the rock directly into it. Of course, there would be loading platforms where ore would be taken off, sorted and bagged. Al moved about sizing up the entire operation. His efforts to steal the ore had to be very clever and he was certain they were aware of most tricks already.

A decision was arrived at to have a regular timetable. And, the first thing to achieve was credibility and loyalty. He gave himself a month. Tomorrow he would begin to play company man and he had to be very convincing at that.

While he ate the cowboy reflected on a place to live. He needed a shack. That was the sensible thing to do and when it was finished he'd sell the mule to pay for everything. Satisfied with that plan, he decided on the things needed to steal ore.

The following day was payday. Al decided that would be a good day to be a company man. If trouble was on its way it would arrive on payday. After breakfast he rode to the mercantile and once inside the tent he approached a woman who was stacking goods on a shelf.

"Howdy mam." Senner removed his Stetson in a polite gesture.

The woman wasn't used to such manners. She grinned and blushed.

"Why, aren't you nice?"

"Thank you, mam, the name is Senner. I'm the new underground foreman at the Mammoth."

"What would you be needin', Mr. Senner?"

"I was after a needle and some thread. I got a lot of tears in my shirts from the brush. Could you get me some?"

The store was rather cluttered. The woman moved awkwardly through a maze of stacked goods calling back to him regularly.

"It's here, just you see. I know I got it somewhere. Oh, sure here it is." She grinned broadly as she returned with the packet of needles and the spool of thread. "It's cotton. . .white alright?" She laughed hard. "It's all I got." She laughed again.

"Laughter sounds nice." Al said. "I know another lady who

laughs. Yes, sir, that's real nice."

He paid for the items. Tipped his Stetson and walked out.

" 'By Mr. Senner," she called pleasantly after him.

Once outside, Senner squinted into the daylight. He bumped into an old sourdough just turning the corner of the tent.

"Sorry. I almost ran you down." Senner stared at the old man. "Say, aren't you Charlie! Charlie Howell?"

The old man put a hand up to shield his faded eyes. He steadied the straw hat on his head as he effected a puzzled look.

"Who's askin'?"

"Al Senner, Charlie. I used to cowboy for McKenny. I met you on a drive when you and Hard Tac was camped near the ranch. We shared some beans a few nights runnin'."

Charlie's grizzled face broadened into a grin. "Sure, son, how ya be?" He extended a weathered hand at Senner. The wiry form stiffened as they shook hands.

Al figured the man was near seventy. He seemed ageless and was as tough as shoe leather. "I'm the new foreman at the mine."

"Well, I'll be. I'm camped down Goldfield wash about two miles. Why don't you settle near my digs? I'd be plum happy to have a neighbor. There's a shed near me what was used for hay before this claim was located. It's pretty run down but it's abandoned. Ifn' you was to buy some lumber, we could fix it up. The roof leaks so you need to cook up some tar and then you'd need some winders'—it gets pretty cold of a night. I'd be glad to help some."

Senner agreed to come down after work that evening. He took directions and said goodby.

* * *

The tunnel had deepened enough by now that Al turned into darkness shortly. Up ahead men were yelling to each other along with the repeated blows of the picks and hammers. The dust was thick. Al coughed hard. Piles of rocks began to hinder his approach to the workers. Muckers were busy carrying the ore to the entrance where wagons waited to take it to the sorters. Behind him men were laying track for the ore cars.

A workman stopped to pull a piece of ore from the load. Al saw him pocket the rock. It took several minutes for the man to resume his delivery where a manager waited. Al called him on it. The man was grisly, shouting and dropping the ore before pulling a knife. Al ducked and the knife slashed at the air. The manager raced towards them shouting to the bulls who hurried into the tunnel. A billy club was used to subdue the miner who fell onto the rock floor with a thud, and suddenly, it was quiet except for sounds echoing down the tunnel.

"Good work, Senner. We cannot tolerate highgrading. It'll be a lesson for the others."

Al watched as the bulls carried the unconscious miner outside the tunnel. He knew they would work him over good. It was a lesson everyone feared. Unfortunately, the bulls enjoyed their work too much. Some of the miners disappeared and were never heard from again. He grinned. This was the start of it and he had a long way to go. Picking up the stolen ore, he put it into his hat and went whistling out of the tunnel.

Tombstone Prospect, June 22, 1893, P. 4, Col. 1.

Parties in Phoenix from the Superstition mountains say the hills are full of prospectors and the ground is staked off for miles around the Hakes mines.

Arizona Republican, June 25, 1893, P. 3, Col. 1.

ANOTHER FIND

Said to Surpass the Mammoth in Richness

The Fame of the Superstition Camps Increasing Daily—Description of the New Location

Few mining camps in the territory maintain their reputation as a mining camp equal to the Superstition. From the day the Mammoth was down twenty feet and pay ore exposed there there has been no reason to doubt the great value of these mines. To add to all the evidence already produced, an additional rich find was yesterday reported that equals if it does not exceed the Mammoth in richness. This location is on a red hill about one half mile northeast of the Black Queen, and about the same distance in a northerly direction from the townsite.

The extent of the vein either in length or width, has not yet been ascertained, but there can be longer be any doubt as to its discovery and location. Mr. White and his two partners in the find have also located a spring of water in the same vicinity and will at once establish their camp there and begin active operations upon the discovery.

Mesa Free Press, September 14, 1893, P. 3, Col. 1.

[illegible]

Mr. Hall and his partner, Mr. Sullivan of Denver, went up to their mine, the Mammoth, early Tuesday morning.

Chapter 4

Revenge

At dusk, Al rode Lady west, away from the town towards the Goldfield Mountains. A smaller, less impressive range than the Superstitions but definitely a choice place to live. For one thing they had never seen an Apache; the Indians didn't come out of the range unless there was a special reason. And since Geronimo's surrender, the Superstition Apaches had been fairly quiet, with the exception of a few raids for food and staples whenever the situation looked promising. The transients and drifters floating in and out of western towns usually used the main roads. It was unlikely, since they would be coming north, that any of them would happen onto Charlie's camp. Senner needed a permanent dig. It seemed reasonable to accept the offer.

Lady's lope along the wash was easy. The cowboy enjoyed the palo verde trees overhead swaying gently in the breeze. Summer on the scorching desert left everyone eager for winter and now that the days were pleasant and the nights turning cool, he relaxed thinking of Katie and pictured their life together. Her beautiful face looming up in his mind's eye raised a satisfied smile.

A shot rang out. The cowboy jerked on the reins, leaping to the ground with his rifle in hand, he crawled up a bank and peered over it. A lean, old sourdough stood spread legged swearing at a dead coyote just below him. "There, varmit, that'll teach ya."

Al laughed hard. Rolling over and clutching his innards he tried to call out. "Charlie, what the hell are you doin'?" He laughed again.

Charlie swung around. "Senner, is that you?"

"Yea. What the hell is wrong with you? That coyote didn't hurt nobody."

"That's what you says'. He was rabid, sure as shootin'. I ain't sure what he had in mind but just in case he was thinkin' of attackin' Hard Tac I cun't take no chances."

Senner mounted Lady and rode up the wash until he saw an opening where they could climb the bank easily to get into Charlie's camp. The old man was waiting, petting the worn mule who had become his only friend. He looked shabby dressed in worn trousers and shirt but his hat, a curled woven straw, was new.

"You decided to come. That's okay. I could use some company once in awhile—me and Hard Tac gets mighty lonesome of a night. Anyways, you ain't the most popular guy in Goldfield. I hear'd that you grabbed some of them miners for highgradin'. They got beat up pretty good, Al. How come?"

Senner smiled. "Don't you know that's my job?"

Charlie rubbed his salt and pepper beard. "I guess it ain't none of my concern, Senner, but I figured you for a different kind of guy."

When Senner didn't answer, Charlie invited him into the shack for a cup of coffee.

An hour later the pair walked up the wash toward the deserted hay barn.

"Well, as you can see, Al, it's pretty run down but a little fixen' will help some. I can help ya'."

Al scratched his head unconsciously. The remnants of a building stood naked below two huge palo verde trees. Its gray facade, weathered beyond description, looked appealing for an old painting. It had a small porch, which seemed welcoming, and the cowboy pictured himself resting there in a summer monsoon.

After they reviewed the damage, they discussed what Al would need to buy to fix up the barn. They talked about it for a short time and Al left. All the way back to the overhang, the cowboy reviewed his options. Charlie was right, he could make it into a reasonable shelter. It would have one room and the ceiling was high enough for the stove pipe. The small loft would be okay for storing his stuff, what little there was of it. He'd make a bunk, buy a chair for sitting on the porch of an evening and Katie could make him a quilt. It sounded alright. He chuckled thinking about this rotten shack which was destined to become his first home.

During the morning, big wagons arrived hauling the rest of the ore cars. It took almost all of the men to unload them but by the end of the shift the cars were rolling in the tunnels. The muckers were grateful. They evacuated the mine to do some blasting while the men gathered near the entrance to eat their lunches. Al moved in. He entered the main shaft to make certain no one was still there; then he made his rounds and paused near a recently blasted drift. The gold was still laying in a pile. He stooped, lifted several pieces of rich ore and stuffed it into a pipe he carried in his hand. Wet clay, laying inside the pipe would contain the ore, which he'd remove later. After filling it, he reached inside his trouser pocket to collect a clump of wet clay. Quickly, he forced it into the open end of the pipe. Within seconds he heard Trooper yell, "FIRE IN THE HOLE." Senner hurried to the main tunnel before Trooper appeared; they cushioned themselves for the blast just as they felt the concussion.

It had gone that way for some time now and Senner was amassing quite a stash.

By month's end, Senner, Lady and the mule were safely quartered near old Charlie's shack. 'Winter is near,' Senner thought, 'A good fire of a night might be welcome.'

It had taken quite a few nights to tar the roof and put in the "winders" as Charlie called them. They did make a difference. Senner bought an old stove in Mesa City which was delivered a month later. He put a stove pipe through the roof and tarred the circumference; the haybarn had become a dwelling. Once it was warm inside, the cowboy decided he had made a good bargain. Being outside on a cold night lost its appeal quickly. His bunk was made from odd pieces found around the barn. He was putting it together when he found the hole in the barn floor. It gave him an idea.

Outside, Lady had a small corral she was sharing with the mule. Since the shack was completed, Al thought it best to sell her to someone in town. Reconsidering, he decided to give her to old Charlie. Hard Tac was getting along in years. Perhaps, he would pass the mule to the old timer as a reward for all of his help.

Later at the shaft, Senner followed the tool nipper down into the main tunnel. The man was carrying dirt filled candle boxes to replace the ones already used to serve the miners' needs of nature. He watched with interest as the man approached the boxes almost timidly. The rats were getting bad of late. Two men had been bitten. Senner used his gun on some of them while a mucker followed along putting poison into the areas which seemed to be the worst in the mine. It didn't help any that they were running into underground springs constantly; water attracted the rodents. Most miners hated them. Senner agreed.

At the lowest level, the nipper changed boxes, then went to climb back into the cage. Al moved cautiously through the last tunnel, the only sound the clanking of the retreating metal lift rising to the surface. He knew Trooper was supposed to be working but so far he hadn't run into him. It was dark. Senner had his headlamp lit. It would hold for awhile, at least, until he made certain no one else was down in the shaft. As he turned into the drift, three miners approached. One of them said, "Well, look fellows, if it isn't Mr. Senner."

Senner froze.

"What are ya lookin' fer"? Some other poor mucker to be beaten by your bulls?"

He glanced sideways for a weapon. There was a drilling bit laying nearby. Senner lunged for it. They hit him hard and he went down. It seemed an eternity as he lay in the semi-darkness waiting to be beaten when he heard three distinct thuds. Suddenly, it was silent in the tunnel. As Senner raised up squinting, a big man appeared and Trooper's pearly teeth registered with a wide grin just above his face.

"Trooper? My God! Is that you? I've never been so glad to see anyone in my life."

"One and the same. But, you see, Mr. Senner, these fellows don't know who or what and if it's all the same to you, I'd like to keep it that way." He helped Senner to his feet.

"Yea. I guess you are right. They'll think I did it. That wouldn't be bad," he said, rubbing hard at the newly formed welt on his head.

Trooper's laugh was gravelly. It echoed through the tunnel.

"Help me load them into the ore cage and we'll send them up topside. I hit them with my drill tamper; they won't be botherin' nobody for awhile."

When that was done, Trooper said he had work to do. He left Senner alone at the drift. The foreman stooped to examine the newly blasted ore—it was playing out. There wasn't even a trace of gold. Senner waited a reasonable length of time and then, rang for the cage and when it clanked to a stop, he pushed the buzzer to signal the operator. Once on top he went to the mine manager's tent. He had not seen a sign of his attackers but imagined whoever sent them was giving them a bad time about now. He would have to be careful from now on. In fact, he made a mental note to buy a knife and to get a small pistol for his boot.

Gillford glared at him as he entered the tent.

"What do you want?" He was surprised to see Al Senner,

The crowd at Goldfield—1894 *Credit: Salt River Project History Services*

Hall and Sullivan's Mammoth Mine in full operation—1895. *Credit: Arizona Historical Society Library*

a man he definitely mistrusted. Hall said he could stay but he didn't have to like it.

Senner said, "I thought you'd like to send an engineer down to the 165 foot level. They blasted a new drift and it's clean. Not a trace of ore."

"We figured that." He muttered. "I'll pass it on."

Senner turned to leave.

"Wait a minute! Where were you last weekend?"

"I didn't know you needed to know." Senner's voice had a surly tone.

"I'm askin', ain't I?"

"I was in town visitin' my girl."

"That's funny cause I asked around and nobody saw you there."

"We wanted to be by ourselves, I guess, you can understand that. . .can't you?" Senner stared innocently into the burly man's face. He had long since learned to keep absolutely stoic about everything. He was alone in his quest. Except for old Charlie and now, Trooper, the mine leaders were a formidable force.

By morning the news spread about the mine playing out. People all over town were talking about the loss. The engineers believed they would have to go down to 275 feet. Hall put the word out. Most of them didn't like to work that deep. There was a lot of water pouring into the shafts. To take their minds off of the problem, Sullivan announced drillers were coming in from the Comstock Lode, the American Nettie and the Butte to have a drilling contest. Immediately, there was wagering. The mine owners put up $1500.00 prize money. All the saloons had pools and everywhere enthusiasm mounted. It would even be a factor as far away as Mesa City and Phoenix just as soon as the stage drivers left town. It was about time to have a party and they were all in the mood.

Of course, the Goldfield money was on Trooper, who proudly prepared for the event. Every few days he went down into the hole to shoot the next drift. When he came out there was a cadre of friends waiting to prepare food, help him practice, give him moral support and make certain he was feeling alright. Everyone in camp was involved in some way or another. Trooper was becoming a celebrity. He wallowed in the attention. Selecting a partner was essential, and the black man took his time. Naturally, men were vying for the position. They worked for hours—each man being timed for his speed. In the saloons stories of the prowess of the other drillers from the Comstock Lode, American Nettie and the Butte were discussed in depth for hours. Each man was telling his own version of what happened in those locales during past contests. Of course, there were conflicts and arguments and some really good brawls. The town never had such a good time; in fact, the mine owners were achieving just exactly what they had hoped. They were still blasting and had gone all the way to 190 feet and still no ore.

Hall was an experienced businessman who knew miners. They didn't need much to set them off. They had been known to pull out of a town in an instant giving reasons such as lumps in the boardinghouse oatmeal or that the pancakes weren't round anymore. He didn't want the best muckers or relievers to leave.

Senner saw it as a great time to increase his stash. There was a small problem: every blast left the muckers with big problems and no gold until they went very deep. The process had taken weeks. For the town the upcoming contest took their minds off of the seriousness of the situation. Senner was privy to some of the meetings and the engineers definitely believed there would be a rich lode at lower levels.

Trooper would blast the cut hole and go back in. After that the relievers had to squeeze down the face into the cut hole cavity; then, cutters trimmed the top and sides. Finally, the lifters moved the broken muck neatly forward into the drift where the muckers would load it into the cage and it was taken to another level for sorting. There were too many miners around to kid the shaft crew. Everyone knew they were blasting and hauling dead quartz.

Just before the contest was scheduled to start, Trooper told Senner he ought to hang around. Senner obeyed. He sent everyone out telling them it would be a big shoot. Senner went down to 160 feet and waited. The earth moved sideways. He gasped. Trooper kneeling beside him laughed.

"That was a big one huh?" The black man's round eyes glistened. It was true blasting gave a man power—Trooper loved it. They climbed onto the cage and lowered into the second level. Trooper shined his light around the huge deposite still smoking with dust. They coughed as they climbed through it.

The foreman whistled when he saw the ore. Trooper laughed and rolled his eyes.

"I'm tellin' you boss, that's the richest stuff you could imagine. Better grab some, Senner. I been around when they hit the rich stuff. You watch they is gonna' get tough with highgraders now. It'll be hard on you—better watch your back."

They both made off with a lot that day. Senner hid some of it down below. He knew he'd get it later, but he had to be extra careful, Gillford was suspicious. Trooper had sewn pockets inside the thighs of his baggy trousers. The gold was heavy. Senner laughed watching the big man walk out bowlegged.

It had been three weeks since the announcement of the contest. People were in town from as far away as Phoenix. The hotels and boardinghouses raised all of their prices making the most of the overflow. People rented out their tents and wagons. It was going to be a huge affair.

The saloons had bought up just about all of the liquor in the territory. Con men were drifting in daily with one scheme or another. There was a feeling of elation and anticipation floating over the entire town: especially when a dray drawn by a team of eight carrying Gunnison granite, the traditional stone to be used in the contest, arrived from Colorado on Thursday late. There was utter confusion as the whole town turned out for its arrival. A rousing cheer erupted. The driver stiffened, drew himself up on the seat, ceremoniously turning the wagon into the square in front of the Saloon. Even the horses were given extra rations; it had been an awesome trip overland through the mountains. Man and beast were bone tired and extremely glad the trip was over.

The whistle blew loud. Its continuing shrill blasts set people to dancing in the street. News of the big hit at 275 feet permeated Goldfield. In the saloons everyone talked of nothing else. It meant the town would survive; it meant work. Of course, there was a big meeting of the mine owners and later, the manager called the foremen in. Senner moved into the room at the mill where the meeting was being held and went quietly to the back of the group. Gillford was speaking in his usual antagonistic manner.

"Now, get this straight. We are building a changing room right outside the main tunnel. Every miner will be examined by a man what does nothing else. The specimen boss' name is Partridge. Any man caught highgrading will face the bulls and then be run out of here. Have we got that?"

A murmur rose. Everyone had expected it. Hall was quoted recently as saying the miners were stealing as much as he took out. Senner smiled inwardly. He had turned in four blatant offenders who each swiped about 50 pieces. Senner took double what every man took on a regular basis. The only problem had been the cache. It was too dangerous to leave in the shack or the overhang; he had been climbing up Siphon Draw every weekend and hiding the ore filled rabbit and deer skin pouches in basalt crevices on the top of Superstition Mountain.

Saturday dawned bright and hot. The late October sun could be relentless and most of the townspeople hoped for the breeze which fanned the desert usually in the higher elevations. Goldfield was at 2060 feet. Fortunately, by the time the announcers finished and the mine owners spoke, a gentle, cooling breeze wafted through the valley.

It would be a banner day. The drilling contest; the party afterwards and the fact that the ore was rich.

THE DIARY OF A FORTY-NINER

MAY 19, 1850 — The pork I bought in town last night is the stinkenest salt junk ever brought around the Horn. It is a hardship that we can't get better hog meat, as it's more than half of our living. We fry it for breakfast and supper, boil it with our beans, and sop our bread in the grease. Lord knows we pay enough for it. When I first settled on the creek it was a dollar a pound and the storekeeper talks about it being cheap now at 60 cents. I believe that if it were not for the potatoes that are fairly plenty and the fact that the woods are full of game, we would all die of scurvy. There is plenty of beef, such as it is, brought up in droves from Southern California, but it's a tough article and we have to boil it to get it tender enough to eat. There is a hunter who lives over on Round Mountain and makes a living killing deer and peddling the meat among the miners. He charges 50 cents a pound for venison steaks and he told me he made more money than the average miner. I paid 75 cents apiece in town yesterday for two apples and did not begrudge the money.

(Found in a diary which was in an abandoned camp near Goldfield)

Chapter 5

Winning The Contest

Trooper was the odds on favorite. There wasn't a person in Goldfield who didn't have a wager out. W.C. White, the proprietor of the Mammoth Saloon and keeper of the purses, felt himself a celebrity. Daily, he recorded the money bet on big chalk boards inside his saloon which were scheduled to be taken out to the street on the morning of the contest. Of course, people were given options on their bets. There were pools for the finished times and place bets on the teams but most people bet on one driller . . . their favorite.

White owned the first saloon in Goldfield. There was no question about its prominence in the mining town and he saw the drilling event as a means to advertise. Early that morning all of the employees were advised how to proceed. Two bartenders strained to carry out the big chalkboard to the platform White had built just beyond the front door of the saloon. Several of the Mammoth Saloon's dance hall girls, dressed in their most colorful costumes, were going to keep score. Just in case there was trouble due to the large purse now housed in his safe, White had hired a few of the mine's bulls to protect the money. Kegs of beer, already tapped, were being drawn quickly while a huge pile of the barrels were layered high in back of the saloon awaiting the onslaught expected after the contest. Ice, purchased in Mesa for four cents a pound, had been hauled in wagons just for the occasion and was now surrounding the beer. Since such a thing was a luxury people came in regularly just to view it. Naturally, iced tea and whiskey drinks would be served as well.

White encouraged a group of the town's ladies to join in the festivities. They were invited to prepare their favorite dishes to be served to one and all after the big event. The competition of the other saloons was evident. They advertised food and drink on huge signs posted high above the front doors of their establishments. Their owners, trying to outdo White, boasted about odds and payoffs. An air of celebration prevailed everywhere. All in all Goldfield was in for a grand jubilee.

By now everyone knew the rules. The team would drill for fifteen minutes and the hole would be measured. The score would then be recorded on W.C. White's chalk board and the whole town could keep account of who was ahead.

At 10 A.M. sharp the first team from the Comstock took to the platform and stood, stomachs sucked in and heads held high, for all the world to admire. They wore sleeveless undershirts and baggy trousers and on their feet high topped brogans. They were particularly muscular and reveled to the cheers as the jacker lifted his sledge while his teammate inserted the bit with a flourish. Of course, the team manager and the timekeeper were allowed on the platform while the two man team performed. Later, as double jacking took place there were arguments about who had to leave the platform. Space was a problem. Goldfield's residents would brook no discussion, they booed and jeered until one of the men removed himself. Everyone was anxious for the contest to continue.

The Capitol and Pioneer Saloons held their bars open. Barmaids circulating in the crowd offered quantities of liquid refreshment which was downed early on. Fights broke out in the crowds. The Comstock driller paused, he was sweating profusely. The sledge almost slipped from his grasp. Cautiously, he stopped to drag sweaty palms across the rag dangling from his waist before continuing when a bystander yelled something uncomplimentary. The driller, a hard rock miner from Virginia City, Nevada, dropped his sledge and jumped into the crowd. It was a full twenty minutes before the fight stopped. In the meantime the crowd hooted and hollered. They had as much fun rooting for the fighters as they did the drillers. Finally, Hall ordered the bulls to put a stop to the brawl and the match continued.

An announcer, Angus MaGill, rode into town four days before the meet. He had taken to the platform when the first team arrived and had tried to speak. The time keeper, a tough mucker, tossed him off the stage just as the crowd began to cheer. His fall was delayed by the crowd who righted him in a good natured way. The feisty Scotsman pulled his red balled tam onto his head in a serious manner, rubbed his nose with one thumb, then climbed onto the platform ready for action. His distinct brogue brought everyone to attention as he delivered information on the first team's final score. The crowd roared. Next, Angus delivered a fine, if not lengthy, introduction to the team from Butte, Montana. Goldfield's spectators cheered them into action. A pair of monoliths jumped into view. They displayed red shirts which fit tight and moved about the platform exposing muscles which had surely been worked diligently in many a contest. Angus called time. Montana's finest lifted a sledge. The clanging began in earnest.

Trooper watched with interest from the ringside chairs set up for the contestants. If his confidence was waning it was not apparent. He considered himself as fit as any of the drillers. Certainly, he was as large, muscular and maybe a trifle younger than the other men in the group. He was also aware of his popularity with the crowd. Nothing brought the man to life quicker than the roar of support from the miners of Goldfield. The women were also paying more attention; that was new and equally desirable. He sat straight, arms crossed, a slim smile playing on his plump lips just waiting impatiently for his moment of glory.

This excitement opened an unusual opportunity for Senner to steal ore he'd already stashed in the mine. He rode Lady around the wash, skirting the town until he approached the main entrance to the Mammoth. Then he dismounted before leading his horse to a concealed spot. He always spoke to the mare while securing the lead to a branch.

"Take care, girl. I won't be long." Patting her gently, he hurried away.

A new stope at the 275 foot level was being worked. Miners hated working that deep, particularly in Goldfield where the earth was unstable. Many of them were talking about moving on. In Colorado, where mine walls were solid granite, there was hardly a worry about cave-ins or timber failures, but Goldfield was another matter altogether. Many of them had already reported earth and rock raining from the stopes as they worked. There was already talk that they might be going down to 700 feet or more.

Hall had offered double pay to any miner working the contest shift. Most men refused. The going wage was $4.00 per shift and today $8.00 wasn't so much considering they had so much bet on Trooper. If they won they would probably get paid a lot more than $8.00 for their efforts and the party was one they didn't want to miss. But, there were always men who would go for the extra pay because they needed it or those who saw the contest as an open invitation to steal ore knowing the owners, the bulls and the specimen boss would be in town for the celebration.

Partridge was a master at catching ore thieves. He'd even made the men strip in the changing rooms then stoop to lift a heavy barbell after each shift. The ones who had ore secreted in their rectums were exposed. Occasionally, someone got away with small nuggets concealed in their jaws or ears some even put gold up their nostrils and stuck clay up behind it until they got out of the specimen tent. Almost all of them had false bottoms in their lunch pails which were weighed at random as they moved out of the tunnel and into the tent. Gold was heavy, it didn't take a genius to catch them. Senner liked to hide his ore somewhere in the used stopes, down in the bottoms of the ore cars on their way to the dumps or in pockets inside of his baggy trousers. Each situation called for different but carefully thought out measures. Of course, he had the luxury of coming and going in the shafts at will.

On this particular day he approached the mine around 9:30 in the morning. The festivities were heating up; there were hordes of people milling around the town. The shift had been down in the mine long enough. They would all have been lowered to the new depth and would already be hammering away at the stope on the third level. It gave him plenty of time to go down to the 65 foot level where he could retrieve his cache. Senner wasn't the foreman that day although he had tried to arrange it. He could, however, claim he was worried about the problems the men had been having with creaking timbers. When it was quiet down in the shaft was actually the best time to hear any unpleasant sounds.

He also had timed his efforts to be over when Trooper began to drill. Everyone was expecting him to win and Al had bet $25.00 on his friend.

The mine was dark as the cage descended to the first level. Senner carried a lantern and adjusted his head lamp before stepping into the shaft. He moved slowly towards the stope which had been closed and where he knew he had a large cache of very rich ore hidden. The passage twisted for a long way until he knew he was near his destination. It was still. The air was dank and fetid. He ignored the distaste taking comfort in the ultimate goal. Every pound he carried out of this labyrinth brought him closer to a normal life with the woman he loved. Once in the unused shaft, Senner opened his trousers and put several medium sized nuggets into the pocket sewn just below the crotch. Then he put several more pieces inside another one on the other leg, two large pieces went inside his hat. He refastened the trousers and started out of the drift toward the cage. Just as he pulled on the cage door he felt the entire area shake violently. The cage rocked hard bouncing aginast the other wall clanking and groaning. Down below he heard the screams of men terrified by collapsing tunnels—their fear rising through the air shafts. The cave-in must have been serious. Senner climbed into the cage and pushed the starter eager to get up to the top to warn the shift boss.

Trooper was well into his second fifteen minute bout. He was ahead and the crowd roared its approval. Everyone was excited. Most of the town was betting on the black man but hawkers had arrived with big bets placed in Denver, San Francisco, and towns in between, for drillers whose prowess was legend around the mining camps of the West. All in all the purse was substantial and many stood to make a lot of money. The black man's skin glistened under a heavy sweat. He grinned. Quickly he swung the heavy sledge and heard the dull clang as it connected with steel. Every tamp was few inches closer to the prize. He was actually savoring his win when a piercing sound cancelled the contest.

Repeated blasts from the mine whistle, screaming that there had been a cave-in, drove everyone to the mine where rescue operations had already started. Senner was the first one to notify the ore cage operator who immediately notified the whistle operator. He made himself scarce, got rid of the ore, then, went back to aid the miners being lifted out of the tunnel.

Gillford arrived shortly after the first bunch came out. He saw Senner and squinted an eye at him. Senner was directing the men to get wagons to take the wounded to the saloons where there would be a doctor and some women to help. They had a first-aid station but it would only hold a few people. Two hours later they sent Trooper below to check on the damage with the engineer and Hall. Five men were badly hurt, two were unconscious and one miner named Stevens appeared to be trapped at the 200 foot level.

"Everyone accounted for, Mr. Gillford," they heard the black man say. "Well, everyone except Stevens. If he's still alive there is so much muck in the tunnel that he'd die of asphyxiation and it wouldn't take too many hours."

Hall climbed up on top of a wagon. "Alright, you men, listen to me. Stevens is in that drift. He's blocked by a ton of muck and there is not much air. Let's get to it. Full shifts around the clock. The strongest men come in first. We have never lost anybody to a cave-in and I want to save him. . . Let's go." His shouts were drowned out quickly by miners rushing to help.

The lights of the town were lit for the next twelve days. Hammering into the air shaft convinced everyone that Stevens was alive. No one could figure it out. "He must have a pipe with him," Trooper told Senner when they stopped to eat the food brought up to the tunnel hours later. "I know about him. He has been caught below before. . .once in Colorado for three days. The guy has nine lives. The big thing is to stay cool and try to conserve on the oxygen. If he has a long pipe he might have forced it up to the blower tubes. It would give him enough air to survive. I don't envy him none. It ain't pleasant down in them black holes."

As the pair rested and ate, Trooper reported on the contest. He told Senner he probably would have won it, at least, he was ahead, he thought. As it turned out, he hadn't won it—the big driller from American Nettie had inched him out. Everyone was so distraught about Stevens they no longer cared except for White, who was stuck for food and a lot of iced beer. As the pair talked they ignored the congestion and noise all around them. By now, searching under the earth for Stevens was normal and everyone did whatever job was asked of them. Miners all knew, except for the grace of God, they might be the one trapped. Trooper stopped to have a cold drink and lifted his head back to sip. Senner was busy shoving food into his mouth and neither of them noticed Gillford approaching. He stood spread legged in front of them scowling as he watched.

"Why were you here when the cave-in happened, cowboy?" he said in a loud voice.

Senner squinted up at him, the chewing slowed. "I came up because the men had been complaining of creaking timbers. I thought I'd check in some places where it was quiet to see if I could hear anything. I guess I was too late. But, come to think of it, shouldn't you and the others have been doing that? Maybe, just maybe, that poor son-of-a-bitch down in the hole wouldn't be trapped if ya' had."

Gillford's mouth drew into a sneer. "You watch your mouth, Senner."

As he walked away, Trooper whispered, "He's after your hide, Al. Boy, I'd watch my backside ifn' I was you."

Senner grunted.

"Besides, cowboy, you musta' got a stash by now. I heerd' tell as you goes up that big mountain every weekend. Is that true?"

The cowboy stopped chewing. He turned to the soldier wide eyed, gaping. "What are you talkin' about, Trooper?" He sounded alarmed.

Laughter curled out. "Ahm' talking about you. I saw you diggin' a hole in the caliche outside of your digs one night when I come to see ya'. I din' say nothin', Senner, cause I din' want no trouble. Ifn' you got a good stash, it's okay with me."

Senner swallowed hard. He was really taken aback. He honestly believed no one knew what he was doing—or if anyone did they were just speculating. Now, a worry grew that maybe others knew also.

He lowered his voice and began slowly, "Trooper, I'm goin' to tell you a story and then, you can tell me what you think." Senner droned on for some time watching the big man's face change with each sentence. He became flushed when he spoke of the day the wagon train arrived at the site. He was angry as he concluded. Before Trooper could exclaim his surprise, the whistle deafened them. Everyone knew something had hap-

Coconino Sun, August 17, 1983, P. 2, Col. 3.

COCONINO SUN AUG 17, 1893

A miner in the Mammoth mine, in the new Superstition district, claims to have sent up $30,000 in rich ore in one night.

x The new mining town of Goldfield has five saloons, and each place has the usual number of games connected with it.

P. 2 col 3

Arizona Republican, August 19, 1893, P. 2, Col. 5.

ARIZONA REPUBLICAN

...A, AUGUST 19, 1893. P. 2 col. 5

MESA ADVERTISEMENTS.

Pioneer Saloon and Gaming Halls,

W. L. JONES, Prop.

Carries a full line of

Wines, Liquors & Cigars

Tables and paraphernalia for all kinds of games at hand,

Main Street. GOLDFIELD, ARIZ.

ALEX TRIPPEL, Mining Engineer and Metallurgist.

ALFRED L. TRIPPEL, Civil Engineer, Deputy County Surveyor, and U. S. Deputy Land Surveyor.

TRIPPEL & SON,

Do all kinds of

Architectural, Mining and Civil Engineering.

Contracts taken for buildings and estimates furnished for all work. Hydraulic and canal work a Specialty.

Office Pomeroy Block. MESA CITY.

MESA AND GOLDFIELD

STAGE LINE.

W. A. KIMBALL, PROP.

Leaves Mesa every day except Sunday at 1 p. m.

Arrives at Goldfield at 5 p. m.

Leaves Goldfield every day except Monday at 6 a. m.

Arrives at Mesa at 9:45 a. m.

NEW COACHES, GOOD STOCK

Carries passengers, packages and accommodation mail.

This stage carries The Arizona Republican, the only daily paper that reaches the camp the same day published and contains the latest news and Associated Press dispatches.

For advertising and news get The Arizona Republican.

THE

Capitol Saloon.

J. J. BIRD, PROP.

—Carries a full stock of —

WINES, LIQUORS, and CIGARS. BEER ON ICE.

Main St. GOLDFIELD ARIZ.

The Mammoth Saloon

W. C. WHITE, PROP.

WINES, LIQUORS and CIGARS.

Goldfield, Arizona

Superstition Mts.

pened. People came from everywhere to learn the news. Gillford climbed up onto the wagon bed. He yelled for silence. "We hit a snag. He's still alive. . .but he's mighty weak. The shaft we sunk is just to the west of the tunnel he's trapped in. I need a volunteer to go down and try to contact him. The man will have to be lowered on a huge cable, We cannot guarantee your safety. Hall will pay $200.00 to the man who goes."

There was a lot of noise; everyone considered the feat very dangerous. The tunnel had already collapsed. There were a lot of people hurt and the timbering was shaky. Finally, several men came forward. Hall approached them and told them how sorry he was that they were being asked to do this but Stevens' life depended upon it. They needed to tunnel into him at 275 feet. It wasn't impossible and they would be given all the help available but, if the timbering collapsed again, it would probably cost them both their lives.

A decision was reached and a friend of Sullivan's, who had come to the territory with him from Colorado, offered to go. Senner watched him latch onto the cable then be lowered. It became very quiet as the creaking cable moved slowly down.

Senner moved into the darkness. He was sorry about Stevens but feeling very disgruntled that he hadn't been able to see Katie. Considering that this matter was upsetting the whole town and he wouldn't be missed, he climbed onto his horse and left.

It was almost morning by the time he reached her. He slipped up the stairs and rapped lightly on her door. Katie stirred and called out softly, "Who's there?"

"Don't be frightened, honey, it's me—it's Al."

She jumped up, opened the door and drew him close to her. His arms felt delicious as he squeezed her inside of them. They kissed for a long time, neither of them wanting the closeness to end. For Senner it was renewal. His whole existence depended on fulfulling the dream and when he could feel her warmth, he knew it was real. He thought at that moment there wasn't any request which wouldn't be met if she asked.

Katie had to work breakfast; she told Al to crawl into her bed and sleep while she took care of it. Later, they rode out to the desert and ate the picnic the Chinese cook prepared for them. It was a glorious day. Al told her all of the news from Goldfield. He also told her they were going to be together soon. He wanted to surprise her with the gold when he brought it in. And, the very thought of that excited him and gave him pause. It had never occurred to him when he was climbing the mountain every weekend with several pounds of cobbed ore how much all of it would weigh when he finally wanted to remove it. Just now it came to mind and he looked stunned.

"What is the matter, Al?" Katie saw his face and it worried her.

"Oh, honey, I just thought of something I've got to take care of—that's all."

"You don't want to tell me?"

"You are too pretty to have worries. I'm the man and it's my job to take care of you and the problems."

Katie smiled. She would have liked nothing better than to have Al Senner take care of her and she was suddenly frightened that it might never happen. He kissed her hard and stood. "It's time to go back, honey. I don't want the mine manager to find out I'm gone. I love you, little gal, and don't you ever forget it. Ah'm comin' back for you soon, honey, and then we'll have it all. I promise."

It was late when he returned to the mine. The shift workers were still trying to remove the trapped miner. Senner went to his shack and slept.

Early the following day the whistle awoke the town. It didn't take long for everyone to assemble. They were bringing the miner up in a basket on the cable. Everyone rushed to the edge of the shaft. "Clear out," Gillford yelled, "Give him some air."

Stevens' face appeared; he was extremely pale. It had been 13 days. Everyone was impressed. He'd survived in that black hole without food and water. Most of them prayed; it seemed like a miracle. Stevens sipped at the water and forced a smile.

A wagon arrived to take him to the town where he could be taken care of properly. He was unhurt and had survived for 13 days on just one lunch from his pail and what little water he had carried down with him that last day before the cave-in.

Gillford rode into town with the suffering miner. At Goldfield the doctor took him into a small room behind the office which had been prepared. They bathed him and carefully spoon fed him some hot soup. Water was administered often; he was badly dehydrated. Gillford talked to him for a short while then left to go to see Hall who was in town for the contest.

The door at the boardinghouse stuck and Gillford's boot lunged at the wood. It released with force and he bumped into the mine owner just exiting.

"Sorry, Mr. Hall. I couldn't get the dang thing to open."

"Listen, Gillford, I know I told you I could see you earlier but I want to go over to doc's to see Stevens. Can't it keep?" Hall looked expectant and continued going out the door.

"Well, it's about that cowboy foreman." Gillford's face soured. He was very angry following along in an agitated state.

"We can talk about that another time, Gillford. Can't you see that I have enough trouble right now? That'll keep."

Hall marched away without looking back.

Gillford muttered under his breath, "You're damn sure it'll keep. I know that guy is highgradin' and I aim to get him ifn' you like it or not."

Mine Doctor Hart, giving soup to Stevens
first after he was brought up.
Photo courtesy of Superstition Mountain Historical Society

Stevens the day after his rescue
Photo courtesy of Superstition Mountain Historical Society

Upper left, unknown; C.A. Hall, owner, center;
William Bolito, mine foreman, upper right;
and James Stevens, bottom, 10 days after his rescue.

ESTABLISHED IN 1878
PHOENIX DAILY HERALD

RESCUED!

July 17, 1897 P. 1 Col. 5

Jno. Stevens Again in the Land of the Living.

"GIVE ME WATER!"

Were the First Words of the Entombed Goldfield Miner Who Is Saved After Thirteen Days of Starvation.

Yesterday William Kimball came down from Goldfield to Tempe after Dr. Hart that he might be on the ground to render whatever professional services might be necessary when the rescue party that has worked so faithfully for the past thirteen days, reached Mr. Stevens the imprisoned miner. All possible preparation had been made and a number who were curious as to the circumstances and the final result went up to the mine last night.

Last evening they had reached a point within a few feet of him, so near in fact that they could converse. "Hurry up and give me some water, I am burning up with thirst" were his first words.

About seven o'clock this morning the shell was broken between the workmen and the unfortunate below and before they had fairly recovered from the cloud of dust and smoke preparatory to descending into the drift Mr. Stevens was seen crawling up through the newly made crevice his wan and haggard features depicting the awful tortures he had endured since the afternoon of the fourth of July.

The physician descended the shaft and took charge of the man and though he is seemingly in better condition than was expected at last report he had not been taken to the surface.

Phoenix Daily Herald, July 17, 1897, P. 1, Col. 5.

Mr. Stevens was in full possession of his reason and well kept his bearings and record of time. Though his awful confinement has left him but a shadow of his former self he has suffered no relapse and it is believed no difficulty will be experienced in bringing him back to health and strength. It is estimated that he has lost about forty pounds during his imprisonment. He ate his lunch just before the cave in occurred on July 4th consequently he has been entirely without food. He had but one gallon of water and that was exhausted on Tuesday, July 6. Since then he has not only endured hunger and thirst but bravely held out against a seeming cruel fate, maintaining his reason and self possession signalling with regularity and precision and though withering away kept up both faith and works. When they reached him it was discovered that he had heard the sounds above him and dug up toward them a distance of six feet. Probably no case in this vicinity has ever excited both sympathy and curiosity to such an extent as the awful ordeal of Mr. Stevens and his experience is a marvellous illustration of the resources and strength of a brave and determined man. There is universal happiness over his deliverance and the breaking of the awful suspense.

It was thought best not to bring Mr. Stevens to the surface till darkness comes again for fear of injuring his eyesight, but comfortable quarters are arranged on top as soon as he is able to occupy them.

Phoenix Daily Herald, July 19, 1897, P. 2, Col. 1.

[illegible] through [illegible] path.
July 19, 1897 P. 2 Col. 1

William Kimball came after Doctor Hart yesterday and took him to Goldfield to be in attendance on the occasion of the rescue of Jno. Stevens from the mine. PHOENIX DAILY HERALD

Dr. Hart went to Goldfield this morning on professional business and expects to accompany James Stevens back to Mesa tonight.

Mr. Wallace, who was so badly broken up in a runaway accident some weeks ago, is doing nicely and it is hoped his recovery will be completed, notwithstanding his advanced age.

Jeweler Johnson of Mesa has a new watch ticker at his house. He is very new and all his experience is inherited from his papa, but time will show the stuff he is made of. There is great happiness thereabouts.

A banquet and dance will be given tonight at Goldfield in honor of the men who worked so faithfully to rescue Jas. Stevens from the mine. Mr. Stevens will be the guest of the occasion. Quite a party of Mesa people will go up to enjoy the hilarity.

Phoenix Daily Herald, July 21, 1897, P. 2, Col. 1.

Marshal Hooker received a letter yesterday from a lady in Texas who wanted some particulars regarding Mr. Stevens, the miner recently rescued from the Goldfield mine. She stated that her husband left her some years ago and that she had not heard from him since he left. His name was Stevens and she believes this man her husband. She will be disappointed when she learns that Mr. Stevens has a wife and children living in Colorado and has never been in Texas.

July 22, 1897 P. 8 col 1

The True Remedy.

Phoenix Daily Herald, July 22, 1897, P. 8, Col. 1.

The people of Goldfield last night celebrated the release of Stevens from the mine by giving a dance. It was an occasion of great joy to those who for days and days toiled faithfully to rescue Stevens. Many people from Mesa were in attendance at the dance. It was also in the nature of a farewell to Stevens as he will leave today for his home in Colorado to visit his family.

ARIZONA DAILY GAZETTE
July 22, 1897 P. 8 col 1

Arizona Daily Gazette, July 22, 1897, P. 8, Col. 1.

ARIZ DAILY GAZETTE
JULY 25, 1897
P. 5 col. 2

STEVENS TALKS.

Tells of His Experience in the Mammoth Mine.

James Stevens, the Goldfield miner who was imprisoned for thirteen days without food or water in the Mammoth mine, arrived in the city yesterday and expects to leave tonight for his home in Colorado.

Mr. Stevens does not look much the worse for his experience, but his face yet has the pallor produced by his long imprisonment. To a GAZETTE reporter last evening Stevens talked freely of his long fast and of the state of his mind as day after day passed and the rescuing party seemed to be as far from him as when the work first commenced.

"I am going home now," he said, "and I do not expect to see Arizona again." When questioned on his weight, he said he gained fifteen pounds the first two days after being rescued, and that without anything to eat except a little water. "I weighed 145 pounds Friday morning," he said, "and weighed again this morning and the result was the same."

"I never felt weak, even when rescued, and could easily have climbed the ladder of the shaft if they would have let me. I did not feel hungry after the first three days, and as my desire for food diminished my thirst increased. I believe I could have held out forty-eight hours longer if I only had another half gallon of water when the ground caved in. As for food, I could have done very well without a mouthful for four more days.

"I was not alarmed when the accident occurred, but I did not realize how serious the damage was until I investigated. Then I took matters coolly, and commenced to think what a fool I was not to have paid more attention to the warning given me several times by the creaking timbers.

"No, it is not a very pleasant] experience, and I am not anxious to try it again, but I do not feel just at present as if I had undergone any hardships. I am a hardy man and can stand considerable punishment, and now that my doctor allows me to eat all I want I have no complaint to make. My chief concern is to get to my wife and babies as soon as possible."

Arizona Daily Gazette, July 25, 1897, P. 5, Col. 2.

Chapter 6

The Cache

Al Senner pulled his lanky frame off the rough board bed and began groping for the kerosine lantern on a shelf just above it. An experienced hand struck a stick match; soon a warm glow filled the one room shack. "I reckon it is just past midnight, a might early for my work," he mumbled. He sat up and seemed tense, expectant. It was always that way before he finished his week's chore.

The town of Goldfield, Arizona, alive and bawdy, replete with gunslingers, drunks and whores, wasn't more than three quarters of a mile away. When the slight November wind drifted to the wash he could hear its Saturday-night sounds but they didn't worry him. An accustomed ear strained for any unfamiliar sound. Lady stamped and nickered in the makeshift corral just outside. Al muttered, "Not just yet, girl—I ain't ready."

Stooping, the miner lifted the bunk off the floor. As it came up so did a plank which was nailed to one leg revealing a hole just beneath it. He reached into it and pulled out a piece of quartz; then, lifted it to the lamp. The gold gleamed brilliantly. Senner grinned. This batch was real rich. He sat down on the wooden floor and cobbed the gold away from the rock in which it was encased. He repeated the process for about an hour. Eventually, he reached into the hold and pulled out a deerskin pouch—where he put the newly cobbed ore; then, he jerked

The Goldfield Mill.

the leather ties taut with his teeth. Senner bounced the heavy pouch up and down on his outstretched palm and laughed sardonically before slinging it onto the floor. Highgrading ore from the Mammoth Mine where he worked had become an obsession. He'd been doing it since the mine had started well over a year ago and by now he had accumulated quite a cache.. Cobbing ore was the best of it but now came the important part. Al crouched beside the bunk after he replaced it and scrupulously cleaned the remains into a pail. He wiped the floor of any dust, and tossed a horse blanket over the spot, eager to start out of the shack but reconsidered the late November air first and pulled on his poncho. Once outside he moved with stealth, disappearing into the wash until he approached a preordained spot where he hunted for the hole he had prepared and quickly dumped the quartz dregs into it. Al's old boot stamped at the earth. Following that action, some palo verde branches were pulled over the spot before the miner returned to his house. Completing the routine lifted his spirits. He glanced up at the position of the moon and decided it had to be nearly one A.M.—'time to be movin' on.' Within two minutes he and Lady crept into the wash away from town headed for Siphon Draw.

It usually took about an hour to cover the distance from his shack to the foothills of Superstition Mountain and once he rode up to the base he could see the lights of Goldfield plain. Occasionally, he heard gun shots, even the piano seemed to filter through the stillness mingled with lonesome coyote wails.

Senner dismounted and tethered Lady. The horse knew her role in the surreptitious plot. She stood at attention almost smiling as Senner gave her a carrot before departing. "You wait, girl, I'll make it as fast as I can."

The climb was never bad until it neared the top. It took over an hour because of the steep cliff face. There was another way up where he might have ridden Lady up a narrow, dangerous trail but it would have taken almost a day to get to it. Since Senner knew most folks wouldn't try to climb the cliff's face, he figured it was safe. Near the top he had to get onto all fours and inch the Winchester rifle along in one hand. Eventually, he mounted the summit and rolled onto the mesa, heaving a huge sigh and puffing noticeably. He always laid there a minute or two to catch his breath while glancing over the edge, appreciating the height and the difficulty of the feat. It was too dark to see Lady, she was behind a boulder in the shadows, but he could see Goldfield's tawdry facade clearly. Up here the sound of cowboys and miners carried. There were more shots and some screaming. Since there wasn't any law just about anything was okay and it usually happened, especially on Saturday after the miners were paid. Last week there had been a lynching at Government Wells in one of the two big cottonwood trees. Some broke prospector had stolen a horse and tried to make off with it from the saloon. Senner didn't go but he sure heard about it at the mine's shift change the next day. It had been the high point of the mucker's Saturday night.

Shortly, Senner was afoot, moving quickly across the face of the big, almost barren mesa. Up here there was enough light to pick his way toward the trees. There were only three of them. The seeds were probably carried in the feces of an eagle, or one of the big hawks whose soaring bodies had always interested him as he rode the fences when he was punching cows. Senner called them Superstition pines and marveled at their spires which pierced the sky up some 30 feet. They welcomed the lone figure moving silently toward them. He used them as a benchmark and once he neared them felt a thrill. Just forty feet away, hidden in one of the pocked crevices dotting the moon-like landscape, was his cache. He knelt anxiously and pulled at the cover rocks to expose the deerskin pouches all lined up in a row, sandwiched between basalt. He counted them to make certain they were all there. Then, he placed the new one inside; patted it confidently and chuckled into the silence of that lonely place before replacing the rocks. In an instant he was ready to return but had an after-thought. He went back to his cache and reopened one of the bags to remove four good sized nuggets. A sly smile grew on his thin lips, "Katie," he said aloud in that desolate spot. "Yes, sir, I'll buy her somethin' real nice." That thought pleased him, he whistled 'Git A Long Little Dogie' all the way back to the precipice.

On the way down Senner mused his plight. He had better than a thousand pounds of ore. . .pure gold. It was 1894 and gold was worth $22.00 an ounce, so the cache would bring maybe two hundred and twenty thousand dollars worth or better when assayed. He shook his head incredulously. He had been so intent on highgrading that soon it became second nature to steal the ore and he had never dreamed he would accumulate this much. He decided to quit'—'hell,' he rationalized, he could do everything he'd ever planned with that much. "But, it won't be easy to move it," he said out loud and then, realizing what he had just uttered, he gasped.

The trip down was uneventful as usual. Lady snorted when she heard him coming; they were friends. That horse knew the game and was as loyal as any friend he'd ever had, although there had not been many of those. Senner was a loner by nature. He didn't trust many people and those he had usually let him down. Considering that fact, Senner put the nuggets into a small pouch hidden under the cantle of Lady's saddle. If he got caught they would never find it.

It was almost four when he mounted the horse and close to four-thirty when he sauntered up the wash after having rode hard. It wouldn't do to be caught coming back in daylight and although the dark dawn was comforting something seemed wrong. Lady snorted and balked at the bend in the wash. Al felt a surge in his gut. Quickly, he jerked at the rein trying to pull Lady around but something held her. He glanced down and two of the mine bulls had his rein. Lady reared. The bull pulled a gun.

Senner yelled in a panic, "Don't shoot her!"

"Then climb down offn' her," one of them yelled.

Senner obeyed. They clutched him on either arm and dragged him inside the shack. It was getting light. Gillford wanted protection in case Hall raised a fuss. The Sheriff from Mesa City, his deputy, and the mine manager waited inside. They had torn the place apart. It looked really terrible.

Anger fused into his blue eyes; he swore.

"Where is it?" Gillford demanded.

"Where is what?" Senner growled.

"The gold. I know you've got it."

Senner said, "There ain't no gold. . .you searched. . .I told you there ain't."

The deputy hit him with a billy club. Senner groaned and fell to the floor. He was out for minute or two. He heard them discussing whether to kill him as he came to.

"Get up," he was commanded but he couldn't. Two powerful arms dragged him to his feet. He felt a searing pain in the back of his head but he couldn't lift a hand to it. He felt warm blood oozing down his neck. They hit him again. This time he was out for a long time. Each time they questioned him and hit him. He never spoke. Finally he awoke and he was sitting in a chair.

Gillford said, "Scum, you better be off this property within three hours of we'll bury you in the mine sump."

Senner could barely see them through swollen eyelids. It was dreamlike and the pain was incredible. The deputy had cracked a gun barrel across his left arm below the elbow and he heard it break. It was swelling bad and he couldn't move it. He passed out and fell onto the floor where he lay in a crumpled, broken heap.

"Senner, you alive?"

It was Charlie Howell. "Senner, speak to me or grunt."

He fluttered his eyelids but they seemed glued. A cold rag mopped at his skin. It felt good. He moaned but couldn't speak.

"Look, you need a doc. You are all smashed up. Hell, I don't know what to do. I splinted that arm with some palo verde branches and tied rags around them but that needs to be set.

I put some horse smear on your cuts. . .it looks like shit but it'll stop the infection until you get to a doc. But, Al, it's five hours to Mesa City. Do you think you can make it? I'll get Lady and put you on her before them bulls come back here. I know next time they'll kill you."

Charlie was as tough as an old mule. His grunts echoed in the wash as he dragged, pulled, pushed and lifted the unconscious form of Senner to the horse who had responded to Charlie's whistle.

Lady drifted out of sight, hid up the wash until the noise at the cabin stopped. When she heard Charlie's call, she sauntered in and stood stiff legged as Charlie struggled to put the lanky Senner up into the saddle. The old sourdough then tied the cowboy on. He led Lady out into a wash which opened towards Mesa City, talking to her in genuine tones about how important her job was. Eventually, the old man smacked her on the flank, calling after her, "Do good, Lady. Take Al to Katie. He needs a doc bad." Charlie had talked to the horse all the while, never knowing what the animal would do, or if she understood, but Senner always bragged on Lady so much Charlie figured it was worth a chance. The old man would have taken him, but his burro, Hard Tac, was old and sickly. At this moment Charlie truly regretted refusing the mule Al Senner tried to give him in return for helping him build his shack.

Senner rode for a long time just flopped over the saddle. He was parched and the pain seared through his body; eventually it brought him around. Lady stopped and Senner reached for the canteens tied to the saddle horn. Charlie had thoughtfully put a bottle of booze next to them. It was in a burlap on a rope. Senner swigged at the rotgut whisky, groaned loudly as it burned the cuts and prayed for speed while it deadened the pain. It even helped him to think some.

"Where the hell am I?" he mumbled incoherently. Trying to open one eye was very tough. He forced himself. He could see the main mountain where he stashed the gold and he was to the south-west of it.

'Good,' he thought, 'They won't look for me here. They probably thought I wouldn't be able to get onto my horse until night and then, they would follow me. They would think I'd go back for the gold and they'd get it.' He tried to grin but his lips were swollen and split. It hurt. Gazing at the sky, he decided it must be late morning. Where would he go—where would he be safe? They'd search, them bulls loved to beat guys; it was their pleasure; Senner gritted his teeth. Everyone knew what they did to high-graders. It was the risk you took when you worked in the mine, and the Mammoth was the richest of all. He was hurt—that was sure—but, he was alive and he had the gold—and if his luck held he'd have Katie too. If he could have yelled he would have.

For a time Senner wandered aimlessly. He was almost delirious from the beating and he was quite drunk. Lady performed well. The horse protected him carefully, treading lightly on even ground and keeping a glistening eye out for rattlers. It was pleasant weather in November, just the kind of day the Mohaves would pick to slither out in the sun for a good bask. If they hadn't killed for food in awhile, the horse would get the full load of venom; in that case, Senner would be dumped off and probably share the horse's fate. They were known to travel in pairs. The miner certainly could not get up to run away. Man and beast kept off the trails and moved further away from the Superstitions.

By nightfall Lady stopped at a cattle watering hole. She had deliberately tried to find one; there had been no feed for over a day now, except a few oats which Senner had given her earlier, but she was parched. They stayed there a long time while the animal quenched her thirst. Finally, she lifted the shiny black head and whinnied joyfully. The sound pulled at the miner's mind. He moaned softly and slid easily from the saddle into a mound of soft caleche next to the hole. The fall stirred him; he opened his unseeing eyes. It was many hours later in the half lit night when he actually came to.

"Lady—Lady, where are you, girl?" The horse stamped and whinnied softly. Senner sighed, relieved that the animal was near. His head ached, a throbbing in his left arm tortured his being and all over body soreness reminded him of the beating. That thought elicited a grunt before he became aware of the mud and raised his right arm to see if there was water in the tank. A bruised shoulder moved him forward until his face dropped into the pond and he felt its soothing coolness.

The horse stepped into the tank protectively and approached her master nickering softly. Senner lifted his head, nodding slowly as he tried to mouth some words. He couldn't speak but Lady knew. Lady pulled at his shirt with her teeth, trying to drag the man from the danger of the water. Senner realized what was happening, he reached up and clutched a stirrup with a crazed expression. The horse moved off, dragging him to a safe place. 'Good girl,' he thought. That effort spent his energy. He went immediately unconscious.

By noon the following day the man opened his eyes. Sunlight and heat plagued him and a few horse flies buzzed nearby, tormenting the loyal animal, who stamped continually while swishing her tail. Clutching at a palo verde branch, Senner tried to get up. The horse moved closer; they helped each other. 'Good old Charlie, he put jerky into my saddle bags.' The horse stood firm, Senner leaned on her lifting the canteen with his one good arm and sighing heavily as the water refreshed his parched throat. The jerky was hard to chew with swollen lips but it began to fill the void. His head really hurt but he imagined the rotgut whiskey did that; the arm seemed so swollen it was unreal, but Charlie's crude splint certainly helped to keep him from screaming. The back of his head had caked and was covered with the black smear, it gave him a real headache, but his face hurt for no reason that he knew, except, they must have also beaten his face. An hour later he felt strength from the jerked meat he ate. It improved him somewhat. He gave some to Lady who was really empty. Senner drank some whiskey now on a regular basis; there was no use suffering if he didn't need to.

He moved toward the tank to flush some water over his head after which he struggled to mount the horse. Lady stooped, lowering the saddle to help him—Senner hugged her long neck and climbed into it. They moved off toward Mesa City where Katie would take him into her loving arms. 'Yes, that would make him better.' The ride seemed interminable and the miner was suffering. His arm hurt bad and it looked purple now and unreal. He tried not to look at it or think about it. Somehow he had made a mistake in his directions, there was no town where he knew it to be. He glared back at the Superstitions, how could be make such a mistake? Was he losing his mind? He tried desperately to think but his head hurt so bad he couldn't. They came to a river and he knew he wasn't in the right place. Lady lowered again and the big man collapsed into a semi-conscious state.

Senner saw her. God, she was beautiful and she was coming toward him, her arms were outstretched and she called him by name. It was the night they'd met in the dining room of the Pioneer Hotel in Mesa City in the Arizona Territory. "Katie is her name. . .Katie Calvert. . .isn't she just about the most beautiful redhead you ever laid eyes on?" some cowboy had said. Senner nodded. He remembered she was wearing a blue dress the color of an Arizona sky, and a white apron with lace on it. Handmade, she told him later. Her eyes were the color of emeralds and they sparkled when she laughed. Senner told her right off he was gonna' marry her. Katie laughed. Senner got mad and said, "Why not?" Katie answered, "Listen, Al, every miner, drifter, prospector and cowpoke said those same words to me. I'm 25 years old, and the man who gets me is going to give me a decent life." Senner kept saying over and over into the air, "Katie, wait, I got gold, Katie, a lot of it." He lost her face and it troubled him deeply. "Wait! Don't go away. . .please, Katie, I'm here."

The next day Senner's state of mind was neither in or out of reality. Lady licked his face, he opened his eyes but nothing seemed in place. He could hardly focus and the pain was acute. Somehow he got onto the horse and they moved South.

Time passed without marking it. He would never know where he went or why. Each day he was sicker, more feverish, more delirious—he saw old faces. He spoke to some of them but he didn't know if they were real. He saw the old farm where he grew up. He heard his uncle's gruff voice commanding him to get out to the stable to work. He saw himself in the hayloft forking the hay into the big wagon parked below. There was a dog named Pard who was his constant companion. He actually saw the cemetery where they buried his mother after she got the fever. Senner was 15 then, and soon after he left to go to Arizona Territory to punch cows on some ranch. He loved the range; it was free. It didn't pay much but one night he put his whole $10.00 gold piece into the Faro game and won. Senner grinned in his confused mind. . .he had almost $500.00. . .a stake they called it. That's when he went gold searching and met the prospectors.

Days later the horse stumbled into a yard on the edge of the town of Florence. They were almost 30 miles from Goldfield. It was five A.M. There was a sign on the door which neither of them could read. . .Dr. Amos Basset. Lady was drawn to a horse trough in the side yard. She drank until she swelled; but, as Lady leaned into the water, her passenger slipped out of the saddle and onto the dirt.

Chapter 7

Doctor Basset

Doctor Amos Basset awoke in the front bedroom of the house in Florence, Arizona. Wide brown eyes drifted from the crocheted canopy and the pictures on the plastered walls to a big overstuffed chair by the tiled fireplace. It seemed quite unreal for someone of his means to be living so well. Hiking up and leaning against the hand-carved headboard, Amos pulled a patchwork quilt up under his bearded chin. A grin surfaced. One could sleep very well in this elegant bed even though he still felt as though he didn't belong in such grand surroundings. Doctoring at Forts in the West had offered the young physician a beginning. He intended, if the fates allowed, to become a surgeon; the stopover at the Silver King Mine was purely pragmatic. Then, after only a few days when the mine manager was taken ill, he was summoned to this very house. The smile broadened on his comely face. . . remembering how he had been asked to doctor its owner. That kindness, which saved the man's life, resulted in Amos' inheriting the place upon the owner's untimely death. It still seemed strange. He had only been here for less than a month but after living in a one room board house at the mine this was definitely a change for the better.

The doctor arrived in the Arizona territory in November of 1892. He had entered the Army just after medical school hoping to move West. A letter which arrived before Amos Basset

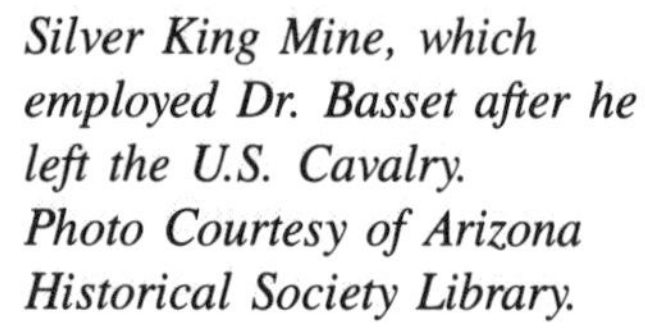

Silver King Mine, which employed Dr. Basset after he left the U.S. Cavalry. Photo Courtesy of Arizona Historical Society Library.

left Fort Whipple in Prescott where he had been sent during the Indian uprisings, said the doctor at the Silver King Mine, near Florence, Arizona, was retiring and the mine was in need of a replacement. It seemed reasonable. Amos was just ready to muster out. He felt trapped at the forts.

The trip to the mine on horseback took several days. Amos was saddle sore and weary when he arrived. Shortly, he learned that the mine manager had been taken ill. He was asked to come to their home and they took Mrs. Mason's buggy. It was a long ride during which Amos listened attentively as the woman described her husband's symptoms. It sounded as if Mason had pneumonia. Of course, it took some time for the patient's recovery. And since they were working together, Amos and Mrs. Mason, Loretta as she preferred to be called, became acquainted.

He admired the house which seemed exceptionally fine for the area and the time. Loretta Mason explained that she was the only surviving relative in her family. He father had obviously adored her and when she came West he wanted her to be comfortable. The house the old man built was big and roomy and beautifully furnished. There was even a grand piano which had been shipped from St. Louis. Mrs. Mason played it for him and he remembered how pleasant the sound was.

William ultimately recovered; Amos dismissed the incident. So, when the Masons were tragically killed in a buggy accident, the doctor was astounded to learn of Mrs. Mason's largess. Amos Basset had inherited the house, the contents, and a sizeable amount of money. Now, Dr. Basset could hang out a shingle in a respectable office and become a member of the community in the town of Florence. The practice would provide stability for the 35 year old man who had only been in the Arizona Territory for a little over a year.

Today was apparently going to be a very pretty day. He got up and walked to the big windows overlooking his garden. It was chilly, early in December, a good sweater day. He decided to go down to the kitchen in his robe and make some coffee. The Pima women, who worked for him, would not be here yet; they never made good coffee anyway. He thought maybe he might get a housekeeper but thought better of it.

'After all,' he reasoned, 'the Pimas were a silent, good natured lot.'

It was surprising to the doctor that these women were becoming very adept at helping him in the surgery.

"No," he said aloud, "I'll leave things just the way they are."

It had been a dream of long standing to become a surgeon. In fact, after he left medical school in Chicago, it was his expressed intention to keep going until he arrived in Los Angeles, where he'd read that Dr. Marcus Wellman was becoming expert in new techniques. They'd corresponded briefly. The good Doctor had even suggested to Amos that he would be welcome to come and they might work together sometime. Amos was certain that dream would never be realized now that he had inherited this lovely place and started his practice. He sighed as he tied the woolen belt of his robe wondering abstractly what Los Angeles was like but realizing that he could never go to such a prestigious hospital until he had had some experience.

The big country kitchen felt cold. Amos quickly lit a match

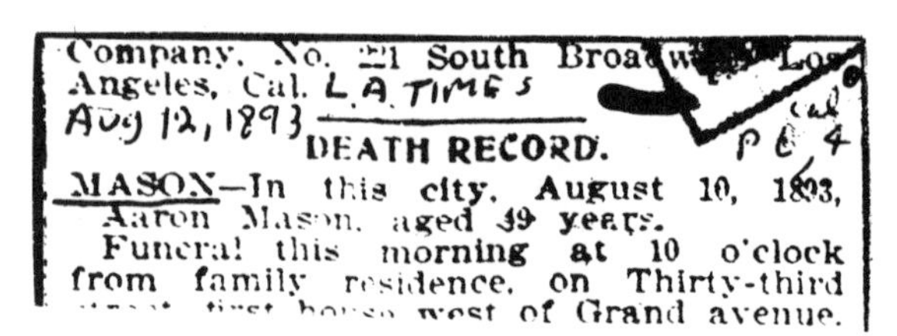

Company. No. 21 South Broadway, Los Angeles, Cal. L.A. TIMES
Aug 12, 1893

DEATH RECORD.

MASON—In this city, August 10, 1893, Aaron Mason, aged 49 years.
Funeral this morning at 10 o'clock from family residence, on Thirty-third street, first house west of Grand avenue.

L.A. Times
August 12, 1893.

One of Florence's better homes (1889).
Photo courtesy of the Arizona Historical Society Library.

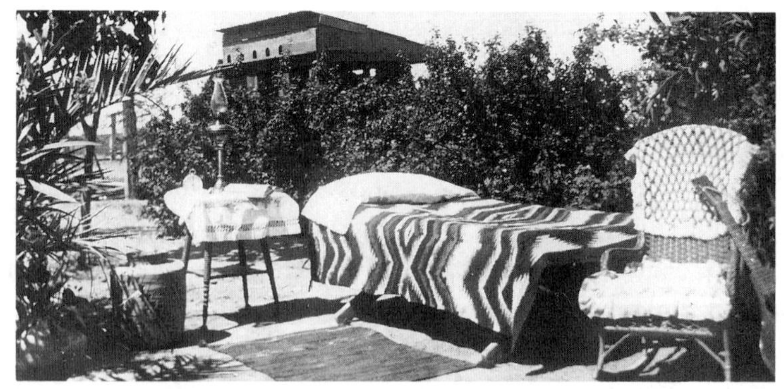

Typical summer evening in Florence, Arizona.
Photo courtesy of the Arizona Historical Society Library.

to a prelaid fire in the cast-iron stove. It never took long to warm, and rubbing his palms over the open round, he enjoyed the warmth just beneath it. The fire rapidly caught onto kindling and, finally, onto the logs. Within a few minutes the coffee boiled on top of the stove. Sniffing its pleasant aroma, he went to get a big mug from the cupboard. There was an apple pie in the pie bin, which a patient had made, and some cheese in the cooler. He gathered all of the utensils, a plate and the food, before going to the table window overlooking the distant mountains. All in all life was very satisfying at this moment. It seemed reasonable to acknowledge that his patient, one Mrs. Randolph Curtis, baked an extraordinary pie. He made a mental note to cultivate that lady.

Much later and hearing the sounds of the Pimas as they neared the back door, Amos hurried out of the kitchen and rushed up the stairs. He did not think it appropriate to greet the women in a bathrobe. The bedroom was awash with sunlight. It brightened the washstand where a pitcher had been left. Amos poured the water and picked up a wash cloth.

After dressing it occurred that since he wouldn't see patients until eight, there was probably time for another mug of coffee. Stepping out of his room, he was shocked to see Juana, one of the Pimas, crouched near his doorway.

"Juana!" he gasped, "What are you doing here?" The woman was ashen. It was obvious she was frightened. He had never known her to be presumptuous.

"You come, quick," she begged.

Amos hurried downstairs, through the hall and out into the yard behind the Indian girl. He was immediately taken by the sight of a quarter horse standing beside the trough. Then, he saw him and rushed to the fallen man's side.

"Quick, get me my bag from the surgery. Then, come back with Pia to help me to lift him inside," he ordered.

It took half an hour to actually take the big man into the surgery. He was filthy dirty and had to be bathed and changed before anything could take place. This was serious, the patient's arm was gangrenous. While the woman helped Senner, the doctor prepared his instruments. He hesitated only moments, knowing full well the arm had to be amputated; there was nothing else to do; the man was unconscious and probably had been for some time. In fact, Amos wondered why he was still alive.

"Sometimes some unknown desire will keep a man like this going," Amos murmured, "Well, Mr. whoever you are, if we're lucky I can save your life."

The operation took a long time. Pia dropped ether onto the cup-like cloth which covered Senner's nose and lips. The woman carefully refused to breathe—except at brief intervals when she would turn away to gulp some air.

The patient seemed to be sleeping peacefully but the truth was he had never regained consciousness. Finally, it was over, The doctor was sweating noticeably. Juana wiped his brow as she had been instructed. Concern registered on the doctor's face but he knew he had done everything he could do for his patient. Now, they would begin the long vigil.

Getting outside seemed suddenly very important. Amos stepped into the garden, taking huge gulps of air just to rid his nostrils of the ether and the smell of dying flesh. It was then he saw the horse patiently waiting and hurried to her. "Sorry, girl. You must be very tired and very hungry." Taking the lead, the doctor pulled Lady to the barn where he removed the saddle and halter. The horse nickered loud. "I know you must have hated having that on for so long. Here, get into that hay and when you are fed I'll clean you up." Amos patted her flank and left the horse chewing contentedly.

The patient was lifted on a blanket to an immaculate bed in a small room adjoining the surgery. He was the color of the sheets. Wondering aloud if the patient would live the night, Amos sighed and shook his head. What a pity for such a good looking young man to die. The doctor guessed his age to be 34 or 35, no more. He looked terrible. But, once shaved and fed, he

Arizona Daily Gazette, October 18, 1893, P. 5, Col. 1.

ARIZONA DAILY GAZETTE
OCT 18, 1893 P. 5 col 1

* A post office has been established at Goldfield, with James S. Patterson as postmaster.

could emerge quite handsome. A lot of time would pass before they spoke even if the cowboy did live. Amos would have to drug him with laudanum to keep the pain down. The women took turns watching after the patient and Amos went down to the barn to see to Lady.

For the rest of the day, that entire night, and part of the next, they observed the sleeping patient. Finally, on the following afternoon Senner moved his eyelids. Pia came to get the doctor. They were quiet but Amos spoke with a firm, assuring voice.

"Please, do not be frightened. You are in a doctor's surgery and I was forced to amputate your left arm below the elbow. You had gangrene. If I had not taken the arm you would have died. Do you hear me?"

Senner saw only a blur in front of him. It seemed to be a man in a frock coat and a string tie. He had a pleasant face as it came into focus but the words were lost on him.

"Where am I? What is this place? Did I die out there... no...I'm in a clean bed.Where is Katie...maybe, she brought me here. I feel so fuzzy...like I'm drunk but different. Where is Lady?"

It seemed like a dream for the big man. In a few minutes he fell asleep again and slept for a long time.

The doctor nodded to the women to let him sleep. He left and took the buggy to visit another patient for an hour.

During the following week, the patient seemed to be alert. He spoke little, only responding to questions about his food or health. The doctor felt certain he was tending to a wanted man. Why else would someone be so cautious? He rarely looked at the place where his arm used to be. That was not uncommon.

Amos remembered treating mine accident cases; men felt diminished when they weren't whole anymore.

One evening during the second week, the patient seemed to want to get up. Amos handed him a robe.

"Here, put this on and there are some old slippers under your bed. Perhaps, you would enjoy a change of scenery."

After having made the offer, the doctor disappeared into his study which was on the other side of the kitchen. Much later he heard footsteps approaching. He called out.

"Hello, I'm in the study. I was just going to get a cup of coffee—care to join me?"

Senner moved slowly. He was very weak. The offer sounded genuine and this man had been very good to him. Appearing in the doorway of the study, Senner leaned on the jamb.

"Are you okay? You might get light headed and I don't want you to fall down. Come in and sit in my armchair. I'll get us some coffee and be right back.

Senner nodded and the doctor returned. He spent the time gazing around the book-lined room. It was pleasant and very safe. The Indian women, even the doctor, seemed especially kind, people who could be trusted, but Senner couldn't be sure.

They drank the coffee and the doctor told Senner how he found him and what had occurred.

Suddenly, Senner interrupted. "My horse! Where is she?" he said anxiously.

Amos grinned.

"She's safe enough. . .in the barn. . .all cleaned, fed and watered. You will see her soon. Be patient, young man, you've been through hell and survived, although I don't know how. I've never seen anyone in worse condition than you were when I found you. Do you want to tell me your name? I'm not prying but it is awkward to keep avoiding it."

Senner was silent for a long while, the doctor shuffled his papers appearing busy and unconcerned.

"Alright. My name is Al Senner."

"What do you prefer me to call you?"

"Senner is okay."

"What happened to you?"

"It was a mine accident, north of here. I fell a long ways and broke my arm. I guess, maybe, I hit my head pretty bad. I didn't know where I was after awhile and the pain was real bad."

Dr. Basset stood.

"Here, let me refill your cup. Then, I want you to go back to your room. You are not ready to spend a lot of energy just yet."

In the morning the doctor approached Senner's bed. The patient was eating his breakfast and, for the first time, really enjoying it.

"I see you are getting your appetite back. Good—that's the best sign. I think you are going to be fine."

"Thanks to you." Senner offered humbly.

"That is my job. It pleases me no end to actually save a life. You are young and should have a good, long future. I would have deeply regretted losing you."

"Thanks. I guess, that don't sound like much but it's real sincere."

"You are most welcome. By the way, my ladies have cleaned your clothes and they are there beside the bed. If you care to get up, it would do you good."

"Yea. I'd like to see my horse."

Later, Senner was taken to the barn. He heard the horse nickering all the way out as Lady reacted to his voice. In fact, it was quite rewarding to watch the camaraderie between man and beast. Amos made a mental note that this man, especially this man, was a decent human. No horse would respond to a bad man in that way. Now, his curiosity was piqued. Behind that dour facade lay an untold story and the doctor wondered if he would ever hear it.

Juana appeared at that instant. She entered the barn and spoke softly to the doctor who excused himself to tend to a patient at the house.

Senner nodded. He was pleased to be able to search for his saddle. Just under the 'fish,' a yellow oilskin slicker rolled and tied behind the cantle, was the small deerskin pouch. He felt a thrill as he searched—what if it wasn't there? It took only seconds but the bony fingers felt it. Al pulled open the leather draw-ties and dumped out the gold. It lay on the work table—four big nuggets. He grinned broadly; then glanced at his empty sleeve. 'Was it worth it?' He guessed he couldn't answer that question.

By now it was almost Christmas. Doctor Basset took Senner in the buggy while they looked for a tree. It took all one afternoon but eventually they found a small, scruffy, sparse pine. Amos laughed and said it wouldn't be Christmas without it.

The two men had become friends. There was no doubt of it, Senner liked the man and had every reason to be grateful. He was also getting very antsy living in a real house and having almost nothing to do. He would have liked to have read some of the books in the study but his mother had not had much schooling and his uncle didn't believe in it for younguns'. 'My Uncle,' he recalled grimly, 'thought that children were to be used like slaves.' That was certainly the reason he had become a cowboy at so young an age. It was probably the same reason that drove him so hard to steal the gold. Katie was the first person to love him since his mother. And, if she wanted a good life in return, he would give it to her.

Later that week the doctor was busy receiving gifts from his patients. He hadn't been in town long but it was obvious he had been accepted. The packages piled up under the newly decorated tree. Also, there were cakes and pies in the larder and cookies just sitting around on antique plates. By Christmas Eve some carolers came by and later, the doctor got out his favorite elderberry wine and his best glasses to celebrate the occasion.

Senner couldn't ever remember a Christmas like this one. He knew that there was something special here but he also knew he had to leave. Just before the toast which the doctor had prepared, Senner asked him to wait. He went to the small room off the surgery and took a pouch from a hiding place beneath the dresser. After returning, he asked the doctor to accept it.

"Here, Doc. I ain't got nothing else to put under that tree but I owe you my life and this just might repay some of that debt."

Amos opened the pouch and dumped the contents onto a velvet cloth next to his oil lamp. The ore took on the light and sparkled in its magnificence.

"My God, where did you get this. We found nothing when we undressed you. Is it magic, Senner?"

Senner laughed. It felt good, he realized he hadn't done that for a long time.

"It was under the cantle of my saddle. You missed it and I'm glad 'cause I really wanted to give you something of value for Christmas."

"Well," Amos bellowed, "This certainly is something of value. It must be worth quite a lot, maybe as much as $400.00. I wouldn't have charged you so much. But, I sure appreciate it."

Al Senner stood tall. In that instant, he was glad he was alive. He looked much better, the ensuing weeks had brought back his color; he was filling out from the good care and the cooking which he'd almost never had before on a regular basis; and, he wasn't afraid anymore. He and the doctor had several glasses of elderberry wine before he decided to tell him some of the story. The plan was forming and he was comfortable with it.

"Doc. I want you to sit down and listen to me for a little while," he asked.

Amos moved to a settee and settled comfortably. He was expectant. It was obvious the big, quiet man was going to tell him one of his secrets.

Senner began slowly. "I met a woman in Mesa City; her name is Katie...Katie Calvert. She is probably the most beautiful woman in the territory. I've known her for over a year. She didn't want to be poor no more and I don't blame her. So, I went lookin' to get rich just for her...you understand...I really didn't care much. I prospected up near Goldfield. I mined hard after the strike and I got me a good cache hidden on top of Superstition Mountain." Senner paused.

The doctor was silent, refilling their glasses and sitting back down on the settee, fascinated by what he was hearing.

"I gave you the gold so you could see how rich it is and also to repay you. Now, I'd like you to give me a stake so I can take the cache off the mountain and I'll split it with you when I get back. If you do you won't never have to work again. It's a lot of gold. I figure maybe almost $250,000.00 worth."

The doctor looked nonplussed. "How long would you be gone?" Amos asked in a totally captivated voice.

"A week at the most but if the weather turns bad no more than two."

"What about Katie? Don't you intend to go and see her? She must be truly worried by now."

Senner's face sobered. "I don't know, Doc. She's so perfect . . .what would she want with a husband who was maimed? I ain't never gonna' be a whole man again."

"It has been my experience that if someone loves a person they want them no matter what. I think you are making a mistake not to see her. Don't you think that is her decision to make. . .not yours?"

Senner allowed as to maybe that was true but he wanted to think on it some more.

"Anyways," he said, "It don't matter none 'til I get the gold. If I have plenty of gold, maybe it would cause her to feel different. I mean, I promised her that and she would, at least, see that I keep my promises."

Amos was impressed by the last statement. He made a decision to give Senner two-hundred dollars for supplies and mules. But, he assured the man that he was not yet ready to travel.

"There is still a good chance for infection and this time I doubt that you would survive it," the doctor said, knowing full well that his words fell on deaf ears.

By New Year's day Senner was packed and ready to move out. Amos followed his new friend to the garden where he watched the one-armed man mount his horse with great difficulty. He had been practicing for several weeks, but the act was still uncomfortable.

"It'll take some getting used to, Senner," he cautioned. "Be patient and take it slow. You are in no hurry and don't be foolish. Don't take chances, you aren't ready yet. Your balance is off and you're not yet healed. Please, listen to me!" He said emphatically.

Senner grinned. "I ain't used to advice, Doc. I ain't never had any but, I sure am grateful for all you done. I'll pay you back; you just wait."

Amos squinted into the sunshine, watching until Senner, Lady and the mules were out of sight. He walked back into his kitchen and realized the house would be empty without the man. They had indeed become friends.

The following is a
topographical map of
Superstition Mountain Mesa
including the canyon
containing Al Senner's grave.

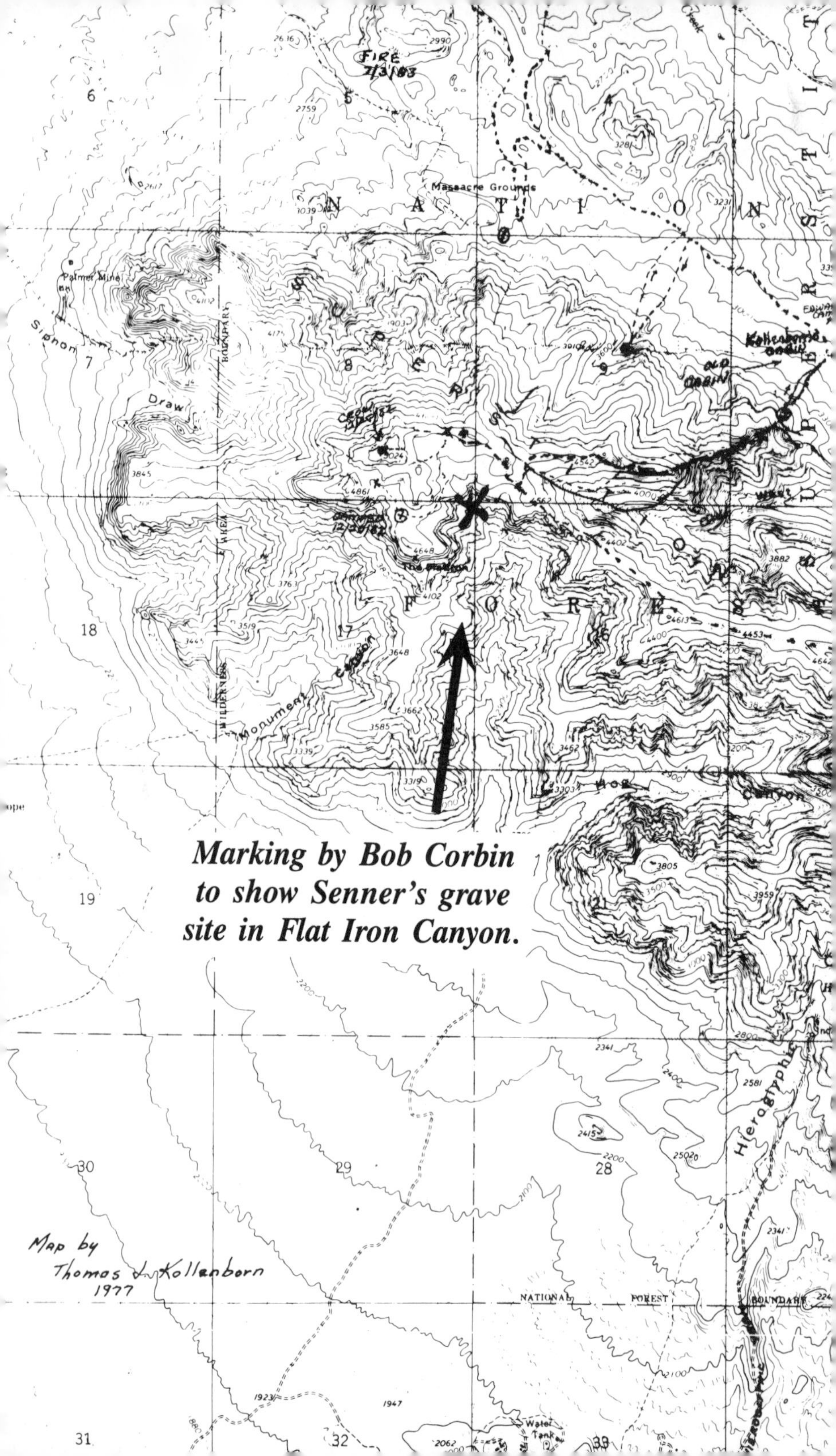

Marking by Bob Corbin to show Senner's grave site in Flat Iron Canyon.

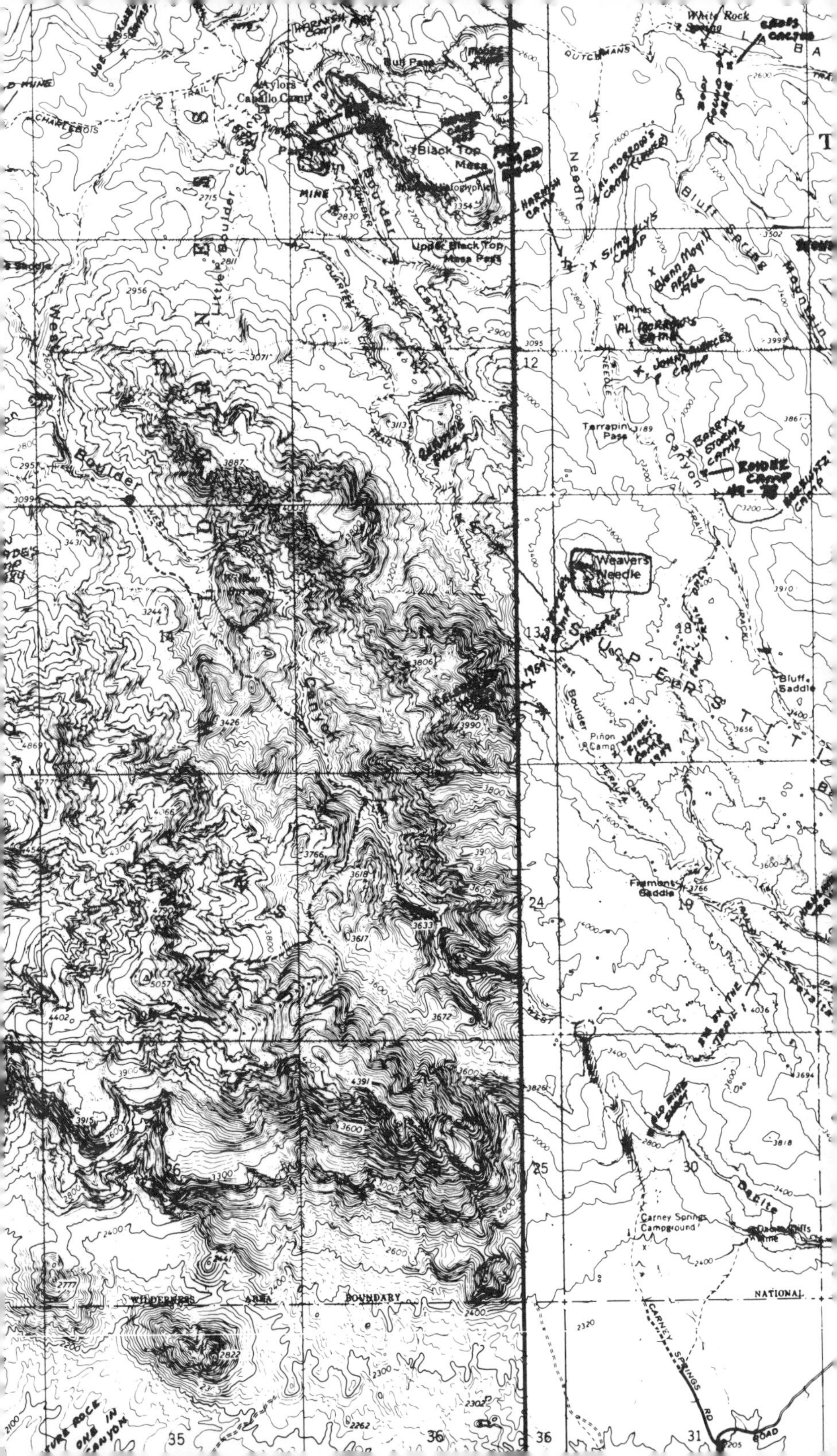

White Rock
DUTCHMANS
Bull Pass
Black Top
Mesa
Little
Boulder
Canyon
Needle
Bluff
Spring
Mountain
Upper Black Top
Mesa Pass
West
Boulder
Terrapin
Pass
Weavers
Needle
East
Boulder
Piñon
Camp
Peralta
Canyon
Bluff
Saddle
Fremont
Saddle
Carney Springs
Campground
Dacite
WILDERNESS
AREA
BOUNDARY
NATIONAL
CARNEY
SPRINGS
RD
ROAD
BARRY
STORM'S
CAMP
GLENN MAGILL
AREA
1966
AL MORROW'S
CAMP

Chapter 8

Her Desperate Fear

Mesa City was bustling in the winter of 1894. All activity centered around the Pioneer Hotel in the core of town which had been built by W.A. Kimball. After becoming the leading businessman, Kimball decided to start the Goldfield-Mesa City Stage Line which would haul passengers and, with some careful planning, eventually also carry mail and supplies. All in all the lucrative venture paid off more handsomely than did all of Kimball's mining claims in the Goldfield area.

It was a five hour trip one way and the mule skinners who had become stage drivers were a rough cut bunch. One of them, Barney Perkins, used the stopover in Mesa City to enjoy some of the Pioneer Boardinghouse's famous food. As Barney always told the gang at the bar in Goldfield, who made a point of tormenting him because he didn't drink, "Ain't no point in talkin' to dumbs. You drink away your gold and I puts' mine in me belly." His laughter was gravelly and resounded all over the bar.

On occasion he had to prove his worth with some drunk who joined in—but Barney, huge belly and all, could hold his own in a fight. Although he'd torn up many a saloon, and was accepted in both towns as a sort of local character; he was, however, a real troublemaker. He didn't drink because it made him violently ill but no one ever knew that. That lesson had been learned when he was an Indian fighter for the Cavalry in the Superstitions. He hated the Army but, as Barney put it, "You got fed, could kill all the Apaches you could find and were outside all of the time." Barney was real sorry the war was over but he had to make a living.

On this particular day the bullwhacker pulled the stage into Mesa City and headed for the hotel. He discharged his passengers on the shaded boardwalk; then, before leaping down, used his big, crusty hands to pull off the luggage while eliciting a few salty remarks. Shortly, he climbed up onto the seat to head to the end of town where the smithy was working at the bellows. He yelled, "HA! HA!" and cracked a mean persuader over the backs of the sweating team. Just at the door to the blacksmith's shop Barney bellowed a greeting before pulling up the reins. The smithy took a huge swing with a hammer and the sound clanged into the crisp winter morning.

"Hey, ain't you gonna' say hello?"

Max nodded and swung at the hot metal a second time. Finally, he looked up, saying caustically, "Barney, what. . .do you want?"

"What I want is a new shoe for the lead horse. She threw the dang thing just a mile out and I'll wager it's a limpin' mare I've got. Can't you see how how that can be?"

The smithy sighed and dropped the hammer, wiping his sweaty hands on an apron before approaching the horse and lifting her front hoof.

Both men were intrigued by the game. Barney grinned waiting for the questions which inevitably followed. The smithy loved gossip and always eagerly awaited Barney's return with news of goings on in the town of Goldfield—which, by anyone's standard, was about as bad as there was in the territory.

"Well, ain't you gonna' tell me?"

Barney laughed, The gravel increased until he was coughing. "It's real juicy this week, Max," he wheezed.

Max went to get a shoe and hurried back not wanting to miss a word. He pulled out a three legged wooden stool to sit on while he attached the shoe and sat down and lifted the mare's hoof.

"Remember me telling you about that cowboy named Senner?"

"Yea." Max looked up. "You mean the one that goes with that redhead at the Pioneer?"

"The same."

"Well, he's disappeared."

Max stopped hammering. "Disappeared! Well, she is still here. That don't make no sense. Nobody would run off and leave her . . .well, almost nobody."

Barney looked up to the sky in disgust. It was his genuine opinion that Max was really stupid but if he wanted to get something started around town this was the place to do it. His mouth twisted sideways. "See, I got this from the gal what runs the mercantile up in Goldfield. She ain't wrong much. She said an old sourdough named Charlie Howell said he found Senner all smashed up in his shack on Goldfield wash. Said them bulls who work for Hall did it."

The smithy had stopped shoeing altogether. In fact, he was turned completely around hanging on every word.

"That gal wouldn't have know'd about it but the old guy needed a lot of supplies and he couldn't pay. He took stuff from Senner's shack to trade. She recognized a lantern she sold Senner because he scratched his name on it. She was gonna' refuse until Charlie spilled his beans and said Senner ain't comin' back. Said Hall told him they'd bury him in the mine sump ifn' they caught him in Goldfield again."

The smithy went to get coffee. He returned and handed a cup to his visitor. "Go on!" It was said with such anticipation that Barney actually laughed.

"What's funny?"

"Nothin'!" Barney growled in an angry voice. He always pulled that when he didn't want to explain. . . it warded off the spirits so to speak.

"Well, I guess that highgrader finally got caught. I mean, I

Mesa Free Press Aug 10, 1893
P. 3 col. 3

Twelve or fifteen miles northeast of the Superstition mines is a mountain which is composed of what is supposed to be chrome iron or mineral paint. There are several old tunnels in the mountain which are ouly partially filled up by the debris of time. Large palo verde trees grow in the mouth of the tunnels. It is supposed that the paint with which the ancient pottery, found so abundantly throughout this country was painted was obtained from these tunnels. Leading off east from these tunuels over the rugged mountain ranges are paths or trails worn down in places over six feet in the solid rock.

Mesa Free Press, August 10, 1893, P. 3, Col. 3.

hear' tell he stole maybe 1000 pounds. They tried to track him many a time, but, he was real shifty and pretty smart. Probably put tanned skins on the horse's hooves at least until he got to the mountain. Rumor has it he disappeared every weekend in the A.M. but nobody ever seed' him go."

"Where. . .where'd he hide it?"

Barney hitched his belt and spit into the dirt. "Hell, I ain't got no way of knowin'. Do you think I'd be standing here chewin' with you ifn' I knew. Hell, most of Goldfield would be tearin' up them hills by now. Besides it's a sure bet that Senner has collected his gold by this time. I mean he ain't no fool."

"Well, where is he? She is still workin' in the Pioneer dining room I saw her in the merchantile yesterday. My Mrs. said she looked fat."

"Fat huh. You must be loco. That woman ain't no where near

W.A. Kimball. Photo Courtesy of Charles Crismon, Director of the Farm & Heritage Museum in Mesa, Arizona.

MESA FREE PRESS
AUG. 10, 1893

ranch. MESA FREE PRESS
AUG 10 1893 p. 3 col. 1

The new brick building for the Kimball House is gradually going upward. It will be a beauty when completed.

fat." Barney was a lech. He'd made remarks to Katie too many times not to know exactly how she looked. Once she'd rebuffed him in front of some of the miners just in from Goldfield. They taunted him for weeks after. He hated her for that and vowed to get even. Today he was exacting his revenge and the smithy was just the start of it.

* * *

The room in the upstairs rear at the Pioneer seemed especially sunny this morning. It faced north and Katie sat in the window on her one chair staring at the big Superstition Range. From here it looked ominous and unfriendly but she knew that somewhere in those mountains was the answer to the puzzle. She glanced around at the empty room. 'Funny,' she thought, 'I used to love this room with the big ceiling and the lovely antiques which I gathered piece by piece.' Her bedspread was ecru cotton, hand crocheted—a talent acquired through the years living in Virginia. The lace curtains were hand sewn and the pillow cases had been carefully edged with a loving hand. Katie's mother had taught her and her voice echoed in Katie's head. "All decent young ladies who are well bred can do beautiful hand work. And when you marry well and you are at home of an afternoon you can embroider or crochet lace." Katie hadn't been happy at home; she left it as soon as she was able. For a moment a grimace formed and then sarcastic laughter, "Wouldn't they die if they knew I was working as a waitress in a hotel?"

"Where are you, Al?" The pain registered in her dull green eyes. There was as much sadness on her face as one could have without actual tears, but she had already shed so many of those that there were no more. It was the end of December and snow was evident in the distant mountains. Katie had received a letter brought on the Goldfield stage the 21st of November. She went to a metal box she had hidden in the wardrobe and opened it. The letter was on the top, now worn from being read so many times, lay staring at her. She picked it up and went back to the chair and opened it.

"Dearest Katie,

I miss you. See you soon.

Love Al.

It seemed so trite. Ten words which meant all the world to her. Katie felt mist form in her eyes as she remembered teaching him to write some words. At first he got mad about it but the gentle coaxing won out. After he learned, he wrote them over and over again and eventually learned a few more. He would never know that no other words ever meant so much to a woman as those. It had been a month. Tomorrow was Christmas and they had planned to go to church together to sing the carols she had taught her man. There was a party planned for the help who worked in the Pioneer Boardinghouse which had just become a hotel. Senner had promised her a special Christmas gift. Katie glanced over at the box on top of the wardrobe all wrapped in paper, waiting. She shivered. Getting up, the young woman walked to the mirror. She picked up a brush and ran it through her long, thick red hair. He loved her hair and talked about it often, even pulling out the knot so it would fall free and he could run his fingers through it. Trying to ignore the pain, Katie pulled it into a knot and pushed in the combs. She smoothed the sides evenly and put on some rouge to hide the pale skin. Her plump mouth curled down as she tried in vain to smile. Soon she was due in the dining room, everyone would be in to celebrate Christmas Eve. They would be gay and people would be coming in to wish her a Merry Christmas. "Oh, God." She fell onto the bed and cried out, "I can't bear it without him."

At 15 minutes to five Katie stood up and pulled the worn red dress over her head. She had made a new apron trimmed with hand made white lace and embroidered on each corner were red berries and green holly leaves. It was supposed to be special for the holiday. All the months of the fall when Senner was gone to the mine, Katie spent hours crocheting the lace and hand sewing her aprons. This one was special. It was for their Christmas. Al was to have had an early snack in the big dining room below and after they would attend the party Mr. Kimball was throwing before they went to church. Katie and Al were coming back at almost midnight to have a special drink in her room and open their gifts. She longed to be in his arms for one more night but now. . . her fingers unconsciously tied the apron strings around her tiny waist. She smoothed the apron, a habit formed five years ago when as a young girl of 18 she'd first entered the boardinghouse to look for work. For some reason those thoughts came flooding back.

Katie had been raised in Danville, Virginia. Her father owned a distillery which produced fine southern liquor. The family had other children but Katie was the eldest. From the first her independence caused her difficulty. Her father expected Katie and the other daughters to learn the social graces, marry well and produce grandchildren. Those ideas were not in Katie's plans. While the others followed their parent's directives, the young woman expected to leave home as soon as the opportunity presented itself. She had been christened Mattie Ann Calvert, after her paternal grandmother. She knew when she escaped from them, which wasn't going to take long, she would change her name and head West.

The hotel was festooned with a big pine brought in from the mountains in an ore wagon. Some of the bartenders took a whole day to get it and even now the waiters and bar boys were decorating it with handmade ornaments, popcorn, candy canes and candles which wouldn't be lit until later. Mr. Kimball loved Christmas and had instructed the staff to go all out. He'd made a lot of money in 1894 and he wanted to share his good fortune with his employees. Besides the party, complete with beef, and chickens, and puddings, and the handcranked icecream, and homemade bread and jams and Christmas punch in huge bowls where everyone could have their fill, there were gifts under the tree wrapped special for each of them. Kimball had even decided to give them each a ten dollar gold piece for their good efforts that year. No one would have missed this party deliberately.

The huge staircase, newly carved and finished, now led into the lobby where all of the festivities were ongoing. Katie would have loved to have walked down it, as planned, where Al Senner, probably bathed and shaved at the barbers, would be waiting in his new shirt which they bought together at the Mesa City Mercantile during Thanksgiving week. Instead, she wound through the worn carpets of the upstairs corridors until she came to the winding wood stairwell leading into the kitchen. A Chinaman named Cholly was sitting on the bottom step drinking some whiskey.

"You sad, mlissey?" he said with a slight slur.

Katie nodded.

"You no should ble, you too pletty."

The woman leaned over to hug the fat little cook. "Thank you. I guess I needed that tonight." Katie brought her 5 foot 6 inch frame up tall, took a deep breath and pushed open the door to the busy dining room just beyond. The room was noisy. That fact and the rush would help to get her through the night. She seated two town folks and received their good wishes with a slight smile. After eight most of the townspeople were headed home to prepare for their children; now, the place filled with miners from Goldfield and a few locals from the nearby saloons. The Pioneer was noted for its food and everyone wanted to see the newly decorated and enlarged hotel and the tree in the lobby.

Barney looked particularly dirty in the crisp, festive atmosphere. He sauntered in, sounding loud and cocky as usual, calling to some of his acquaintances and moving about the big dining room to make certain everyone heard him. Katie avoided him as long as she could, but soon it became apparent that he wanted to be seated.

"Please, take the second table in the corner. It will be cleaned in a moment," she said softly, concealing her hatred.

"Yea. Okay, but hurry it up."

She ignored the burly man just as though he wasn't there but this was her usual reaction to him. Katie walked away.

"I'll bet you want news of Senner." He said it loud and then sat back.

She stiffened. Not answering would have been smart, but her heart ached. Turning, she went back to the table and her eyes told him all he wanted to know.

"He's gone. Di'nt you know?" Then he held up an envelope and waved it in her face.

Katie gasped. "Please, tell me what you know. Is that a letter for me?"

"Wild horses couldn't get it out of me, lady, but, now, ifn' you was to say. . .let me come up to your room tonight, I guess, I could remember what I heard and you could, say, see this here letter."

Two cowboys from a ranch just north of town overheard the conversation. One of them nudged the other one. They approached Katie and took her arm. "Mam, Ted and me was hopin' you'd come to our table for a moment. We need to have a chat, quiet like."

Katie followed, tears welling up in her eyes. They led her to the other side of the dining room where they sat down. She had her back to Barney who looked smug as he watched.

Luke stared at her. "Mam, that scum is what you'd expect from Goldfield. Don't pay him no mind. If you'd like we could have a talk with him a little later. You go about your business . . .okay?" Katie nodded and moved from the room and asked someone else to serve Barney. Later, when the stage driver left, Katie returned to the dining room. It was time for the party to start.

Everyone began to gather in the lobby while Mr. Kimball gave out the gifts. There were presents to each other and food gifts from the cooks and Mr. Kimball's gold pieces and perfume from the manager. All in all, it was a good Christmas. Katie waited a decent interval, then slipped away to the kitchen so she could hurry up to her room.

Once inside she put on a scarf and her woolen cape before leaving via the back stairs which opened into an alley beside the hotel. It was cold this late and the street, usually filled with horses and people, seemed empty. Even the bars were quieter than usual. The church was at the north end of town. Katie pulled the wool cape closer around her body. The emotion of making this trip without Al chilled her very being. Her footsteps pounded on the boardwalk and soon, as she barely noticed the cadence, she became totally engrossed in her torpor. Eventually, nearing the white clapboard building where voices rose in song,

Katie became aware that it was Christmas Eve and she needed to be part of the warmth and consolation that waited inside. She crossed the dirt street. Just on the other side was a path leading up onto a small promontory upon which the church sat. There were wide wooden steps. Katie lifted her skirts to start up and someone lurking in the shadows appeared. Katie screamed as Barney grabbed her and tried to drag her around the side of the building. The sound would be lost on those inside the building who were just finishing a melodious chorus of 'O, Holy Night.'

Suddenly, the two cowboys from the dining room appeared beside her. "Run, Katie—run into the church," one of them ordered as they released her from Barney's grasp.

She fled without looking back.

It was warm inside and the voices of the choir lifted in concert to the strains of 'Silent Night.' It took only seconds to find a pew and slip into it. Katie was still shaking but suddenly she became renewed by the smell of pine from the trees decorating the big room mingled with incense and the burning candles. The music lifted her spirits and for a moment she felt safe and warm. After she began to sing, relief overtook her. An hour later the pastor was saying goodby to everyone at the door. They all clustered around the steps wishing each other a Merry Christmas. Katie looked down and saw the cowboys. They motioned to her.

"How about if we walk you back to the Pioneer, Miss Katie?"

She smiled. "I'd appreciate that."

"He was beat up pretty bad." Luke said as they moved away from the crowd.

"Are you sure?" Her voice choked as she asked.

"Yes, mam. Old Barney spilled his guts after we persuaded him. Senner got picked up by the bulls from the mine. He never told them nothin' but they beat him real bad and left him on the floor of his shack. An old sourdough named Charlie found him and fixed him up and put him on his horse. . .That's the last anybody saw of him. . .and mam. . .there weren't no letter. He just wanted to torment you."

Katie sobbed. They stopped a moment while she composed herself. Looking up at them she said, "Oh, thank you for all you have done. I really couldn't have stood much more. I believe you know the true meaning of Christmas."

They left Katie at the hotel and she hurried up to her room. She knew that this was the worst Christmas of her life and she wanted to be alone. She wouldn't know until morning that Barney Perkins had been shot to death just outside the Red Dog Saloon sometime before midnight and nobody knew who did it.

For a moment after she lit the oil lamp, Katie stared at Al's picture. The photograph was faded but she saw his handsome face smiling at her and cried out, "Oh Al, now I've lost you. Why?" Katie didn't sleep much that night. The rumor that Senner ran off and left her high and dry would be all over town by New Year's Day. Everyone would be calling him a highgrader and a thief because the mine owners wanted the story of his horrible beating to make it around the territory. That beating just might stop the stealing.

Katie watched the sun come up in the east. It was still and frozen outside and the mountains had a fresh blanket of snow on their peaks. Her heart was broken but she would never believe that Senner ran away from her. No man could have been as tender as he had been and not have loved her, but, somehow knowing that did nothing to warm her heart on that cold winter's morning.

Regarding the home life at Goldfield—Goldfield and Bull Dog cover an area some three miles square, and while they are separated in the mind of the observer, they are, for the purpose of this writing, considered as one; and the name Goldfield covers both. The majority of the habitations are built of canvas and palo verde poles. There are a few very respectable looking boarding houses, compactly built to keep out rain and heat in the summer and the cool night air of fall and winter.

The boarding house owned by Mr. Kimball of Mesa and patronized by the miners and carpenters employed on the Mammoth mine and mill, is a neat wooden structure containing two rooms, one for the dining-room and the other for a kitchen. This is located close to the mine and alongside the roadway, which is the main thoroughfare of the camp. Across the road is the general store of Peterson Bros., that is also a wooden building, and the young men who conduct it deserve the large patronage they have gained for their enterprise and faith in the camp.

There's a butcher shop down on the road which is also a board building, and a saloon off in the other direction up the hill, a neat wooden structure. Here and there, scattered about the low hills, are tents and pole shacks providing comfortable semi-outdoor abodes. A favorite style of dwelling is a tent with a porch built at the opening, of palo verde poles and the branches of mesquite and other trees. The porch forms a kitchen, dining-room, sitting-room and in fact the living-room, as the women call it, or parlor as the men jocularly term it. At any rate they are pleasant and comfortable living places for a new mining camp and the housewives and daughters keep them as clean as the ground can be swept. The miners and other workmen without families, are provided with, or provide for themselves, tents and cots. Many of them during the warm weather unroll their blankets on the ground and sleep with the sky for a covering, without a notion of fear of the creeping and crawling insects and reptiles which terrify a tenderfoot. Sleeping outdoors is a common thing and there are many of these sleepers to be seen scattered over the low hills of Goldfield.

The canteen in Goldfield is as indispensable as the Bible in a camp meeting. The miner and the prospector cling to it as closely as does the Christian to the Book. From the canteen comes that fountain of temporal life and without it the traveler is likely to suffer as much the misery of thirst as the sinner without salvation suffers the fear of damnation.

Taken out of a Phoenix newspaper, 1894.

Chapter 9

The Search

By February Doctor Basset's concern over Senner's failure to return mounted. He was beginning to doubt the cowboy; perhaps, he'd been cheated out of $200.00; yet, it was hard to believe that anyone as sick as the man was when he found him could make up a story like that. Amos determined one night, sitting by the fire, that tomorrow he would go to the Pinal County Sheriff's office and file a missing person's report. Having decided that, he refilled his glass with his favorite wine and carried it to his bedstand still musing the fact that Senner was supposed to be gone for a week at the most. He left in December. It was now the middle of February and there was still no sign of him.

An explosion at the Silver King mine consumed his time for several weeks. A few of the miners suffered broken limbs, there were burn victims, especially one old timer whose future was doubtful, and many cuts and abrasions. The entire matter kept him more than busy. It wasn't easy to get to the mine where he spent a lot of hours and sometimes had to stay the night. Then, of course, there were all of his patients in town who expected to have his services when they needed them.

He was already tired and edgy when he finally decided to file the missing persons report at the Pinal County Sheriff's Office. The deputy, a pudgy, unresponsive man, barely looked up at the request and was anything but encouraging. He said, "Oh, listen! Doc, he'll be back as soon as the $200.00 you gave him runs out." Amos didn't want to believe the worst of Senner. He decided to find out for himself. But, as hard as he tried, he could not get away until the 15th of March.

The Pima nurses were going to tend to his home and patients until his return. If something urgent came up they were directed to send everyone to one of the two other doctors in the area. However, a patient appeared before he left who was going to take a lot of time. It was almost noon before Dr. Basset got started for the long ride to Goldfield.

The Superstitions loomed large up ahead and it seemed that they were further away the more he rode. The trip was supposed to be twenty eight miles as the crow flies. By dusk Amos crossed onto the Goldfield road and headed up the foothills into the community center.

The town was bigger than he'd imagined. In fact, he learned later that some 1500 people lived there or nearby. There were five saloons. The wooden structures sat up on a promontory where anyone entering town wouldn't miss them. Amos looked for the boardinghouse, riding past a post-office, an assayer, a Chinese laundry, livery stable and a school which were staggered around the main street. At first glance it seemed almost civilized but that wasn't true. Everyone knew that Goldfield was the wildest place in the territory.

The boardinghouse seemed well run and clean. His room was furnished in very plain board pieces not unlike the one he'd had at the Silver King Mine. He laughed when he saw it. Shortly, as he poured some water into the crock bowl to wash, he muttered out loud, "I used to think this was pretty grand." A smile rose. "Amos, old boy, you are spoiled." After he was washed, he felt better. The bed wasn't really soft but he was too tired to care. He sat down heavily on the straw mattress, laid back and immediately, fell asleep.

In the morning after breakfast, he hurried to the Pioneer Saloon where he was told he'd find the deputy. It didn't take very long before the doctor realized he had befriended a high-grader and a thief. He was noticeably disappointed and then made a decision to stay in the saloon for a game of cards. The ride to Goldfield had been arduous. And, as busy as life had become, the doctor wasn't going to return just yet. During the game, the subject of Senner came up. Dr. Basset's anger provoked the conversation and the locals were only too happy to oblige.

One of them said, "You see, Doc, you've been taken by one of the best con men in the territory. Al Senner sure as hell took you and the Mammoth. Some of the company officials believe he made off with, at least, 1000 pounds of the richest high-grade ore ever removed from the Mormon Stope. Why—Al hiked to the top of Superstition Mountain every Sunday that it didn't snow or rain. Most of us believe he carried his ore to the mesa. I know you can't believe that a man would go to such lengths to hide his cache when there are so many good places down here. But, just think for a moment, five hundred to a thousand pounds of ore that rich is worth a lot of money. Al wanted a safe place to hide his gold and he found it on top of that mountain. Now, he'll be able to marry Katie and run off." He laughed, "Wouldn't anybody do that if they had a stake like that one?"

The doctor feigned ignorance of the woman. As he listened to them explain he thought it was quite reasonable for a man to steal gold for the woman he loved and smart to hide it on top of a mountain which was quite inaccessible. His next question brought an interesting response and certainly explained Senner's decision to put his cache where he put it.

"Tell me, gentlemen," the doctor asked, "Is it possible to ride a horse to the top of Superstition Mountain?"

The discussion became quite heated. Everyone volunteered an opinion: half of them said it couldn't be done and the others didn't know, but, the consensus was that none of them would have attempted it.

An old cowboy sitting off to the side ventured an idea. He

said there was only one man in these parts who could answer that question—a cowboy named Joe Gibson who worked at the Quarter Circle U near the southern end of Superstition Mountain.

Amos Basset was enjoying his respite from duties. He stayed another day and enjoyed a big steak in the Pioneer that night. There was a honky tonk piano player who kept them entertained. The liquor flowed freely which improved the conversations considerably and Amos suddenly remembered how nice it was to have companionship, especially of such raucous, uninhibited types. Of course, there were women in the Pioneer also but Amos knew what kind of disease they carried. He'd decided a long time ago that his profession would be his mistress for now; then, if time allowed and he met the right one. . .he'd marry.

On the following morning he rose early; eager to get started for the Quarter Circle U to search for the cowboy. Being such a serious man, he never allowed much time for fun. The Senner matter weighed heavily on his active mind and he wasn't going to waste a minute.

March blew in with a roar that year. But, after living on the desert for some time now, the doctor enjoyed the brief winter. He pulled his collar up about his neck and wrapped a muffler around it. The wool felt good against his skin. It was quite beautiful riding through the scrub and mesquite in the foothills of the range: the desert smelled clean and the big hawks soaring in the sky were pleasant to watch; there were quail in the palo verdes and frequently, he heard the cooing of the mourning doves. Glancing high above him, he could get a clear view of the main mountain, looking forboding and for all the world unscalable, at least, on a horse. The feat, however difficult, still had to be tackled if at all possible. By now his resolve was fixed; if there was a cache up on that mesa he had to search for it, and the man named Senner with whom he had made a bargain.

By noon the trip was accomplished. Amos Basset, shod of

his muffler, rode onto the Quarter Circle U feeling dusty and dry. A cowboy leaned against a weathered post in front of the ranch house chewing on a piece of straw. He was stocky, clad in old brown chaps, a clean, plaid shirt and a dark brown cowboy hat. His slim smile preceeded a warm greeting and, although the doctor couldn't see his blue eyes under the deep brim, he knew they were welcoming.

"Howdy," Joe said.

Water was offered which Amos gladly accepted. Joe sauntered toward the pump and returned with a big tin cup of icy well water. It tasted like ambrosia. Amos asked for more. Joe obliged.

"Sit a spell," he said.

They moved up to the cover of the porch and sat on the edge. Being a cowboy, Joe knew he wouldn't have to ask questions. Whatever this stranger wanted would be said quick enough. Joe crossed his boots and leaned into the shade still sucking on the straw.

"Joe, can you ride a horse to the top of Superstition Mountain?"

If the cowboy was surprised he didn't show it. "Yup. But it's dangerous."

"Well, could you do it and lead two pack mules up with you?"

The cowboy seemed to be studying the matter. "Yup. But you'd have a tough time controlling them and your own animal."

A soft wind blew over the ranch lifting some tumble weeds which rolled across the opening just in front of the gate. They both watched them silently. The doctor was deep in thought.

If Senner really did go up there with the supplies the doctor helped him buy, maybe there was some sign of him. If not he'd at least know if he had been cheated which didn't seem so important anymore. Whatever the outcome, he wanted to know. He'd come this far and he meant to go on—if he could convince this man to help him.

"I'd pay you $30.00 gold if you'd take me up there."

The cowboy knew that $30.00 was two months pay. "That's

quite a lot, Doc. Mind if I ask why it's so danged important?"

"No. I grubstaked a cowboy who was looking for a cache he had. He's disappeared. I believe he is on that mountain. Call it a hunch; I saved his life once and his whereabouts is important to me."

Joe assured him it would be a tough journey. He recommended that the doctor go home and tend to his patients and live a long life.

"I'll pay you $50.00 to take me." Amos persisted.

It was silent for a moment. Joe knew he'd work a lot of months for that much money. The doctor seemed determined, so—why not? "Okay. But I got to git to Mesa City and git permission from Mr. Marler. He owns the spread. That will take two days. And I don't want no problem if you git killed or hurt. I'm tellin' you it's dangerous."

Doctor Basset scowled. It was quite evident he didn't want to wait. "Isn't there some other way?"

Joe thought for awhile. Finally he said, "Well, maybe I could find somebody at Goldfield to come and stay here. I got a friend. He might do it."

The doctor cautioned Joe not to tell anyone in Goldfield where he was going or with whom. The cowboy nodded and they both knew that was as good as his word.

Amos settled into the ranch house that night. By noon the next day, as promised, Joe Gibson rode in pulling two pack mules laden with supplies. Within an hour they were on the trail, heading for the entrance to Willow Canyon. Once they entered it, they began to climb a rocky trail until they reached the summit between Willow and East Boulder Canyons. They were near Horsehead when they made camp for the night. It had been a long ride and the doctor was glad to get out of the saddle.

Joe made a fire. They spent a lot of time tending their animals and making certain they were in good shape. Later, Joe cooked potatoes, bacon, and beans to go with the coffee he brewed. After a good feed they bedded down for the night. They were

Arizona Republican

THE KID SEEN

June 15, 1893 P.2 col. 1

Near Bark and Criswell's Ranch.

A Cowboy Holds a Brief and Nervous Conversation With the Renegade.

A report reached Tempe yesterday that the Kid was seen near Bark & Criswell's ranch, commonly known as the Marlow place, on Tuesday by Joe Gibson, a young cowboy employed on the rodeo in that vicinity. The exact location of where the Indian was seen was at the water holes, the only place where water is found for some miles.

Gibson had his Winchester in hand and could have killed the renegade or could have taken a shot at him, but fear that he might be mistaken in the man, together with the fact that the Indian was armed with both rifle and pistols, prevented him from shooting.

The Indian was accompanied by a short and squabby young squaw who was also carrying a Winchester. Gibson for a moment hesitated and took in the situation at a glance, and while his first impulse was to shoot, his second was self-preservation and with rifle in hand he rode slowly away, leaving the Indian at the tanks. They had a few words of conversation and Gibson asked the Kid whether four or five men had passed by and was answered in the negative in good English.

A few days ago there was a rumor that twenty-five renegades from the reservation at San Carlos had joined the Kid in the Superstition mountains, but this is the first seen of any in that vicinity.

The nearest ranch to the one where the Kid was seen is the Frazier ranch, where little Charlie Dobie of Tempe, was killed by the Kid one year ago.

While many depredations have been committed and men foully murdered in various localities in southeastern Arizona, each of which has been attributed to the outlaw, those who reside in the vicinity of the Superstitions say the Kid has most of the time during the past year camped in that rough region peculiarly situated for secretion and at the same time a good pasture ground for an Indian.

There seems to be but little doubt as to the identity of the Kid as the description of the fellow given by young Gibson tallies with that of the Kid. Much excitement prevails in the mountains and it is difficult for the cattlemen in that vicinity to procure help as the Kid is a terror even to the Arizona cowboy when stationed alone on a solitary cattle ranch. It is said moccasin tracks may be seen in the dry sandy washes near these water holes at any time of the year but it is seldom an Indian is seen.

Article from the Arizona Republican, *June 15, 1893, which mentions Joe Gibson, a young cowboy.*

"A report reached Tempe yesterday that the Kid was seen near Bark & Criswell's ranch, commonly known as the Marlow place, on Tuesday by Joe Gibson a young cowboy employed on the rodeo in that vicinity."

both tired, but Joe was anticipating a hard ride the next day and he wanted this tenderfoot to be able to handle it.

The sun broke late because they were so deep into the canyon near the springs. There was water running that time of year and the sound of it welcomed Amos when he awoke. Cold air chilled them and they both pulled their ponchos around them, at least, until Joe had a good pot of coffee brewing. By seven they were packed and ready to move out.

Amos followed the mules at a comfortable distance; he had great respect for their surefooted reputation. His eyes looked ahead at what looked like an impossible climb. Joe said they were going into West Boulder but it was difficult to track. A rock covered trail ahead totally engrossed man and beast. Joe leaned almost out of his saddle carefully scrutinizing the horses' steps. No one wanted an animal to break a bone and each step seemed more difficult than the last one. After a long struggle Joe lead them off into a side canyon which followed a westerly direction toward the eastern slope of Superstition Mountain.

They were moving slowly. Amos felt a chill wind blowing down the passage and noticed storm clouds overhead. It was beginning to feel cold.

Joe stopped the train and waved a hand to signal. "Doc, we got a problem. There is a bad storm coming. I know of a cave nearby and I think we ought to crawl in there for the night."

"I don't want to stop this early, Joe. It's only one o'clock." Amos argued.

"Listen, we'd better get to collecting wood or we will have a hard night. Besides, if we get caught out here in the open all our gear will get wet and we will have to go back to the ranch."

That being the case, Amos didn't believe he had a choice. He reluctantly followed the cowboy to the mouth of huge overhang that slanted down above a good sized cave in the back.

Joe's movement puzzled Amos. Joe rushed to store all of their gear in the back of the cave; after that he was in and out carrying all of the wood he could find. By 2:30 PM they were almost settled. And the doctor had started a good fire which felt very comforting.

"There is no chance of making it to the top today," Joe said almost to himself but aloud.

The clouds were collecting in heavy clumps and it was getting colder by the minute but the air became very still. Joe pulled off his hat and rubbed his hand over his hair. "It's going to storm like hell tonight, Doctor. And, you'll be damned glad you aren't up on the top."

"Looks like we never will get to the mesa."

Joe shook his head and grinned, "Be patient, we'll get there eventually. Those rocks will be slick as cow slobber after this weather and if'n we should slip it might just be the end. I don't guess that's what you had in mind—is it?"

During the night, the rains came. Amos awoke just as the last embers of the fire were dying. The few licks of flames shadowed on the huge slanted basalt roof. Outside, the rain slapped against rock and the sounds were somehow reassuring. He laid awake and thought how lucky he was to have selected the right cowboy to take him up on Superstition Mountain. Had his impatience been the main factor and he was with someone less experienced he would probably have been out in the open and wet by now.

While he drank his morning coffee, Amos moved to the wide opening of the overhang. He gazed up towards the summit high above them. It was completely engulfed in clouds and there seemed no doubt, with such low temperatures, that a blizzard had moved onto the mesa.

Joe returned from feeding the animals. He looked stoic. "Doc, I got to go back to the ranch to see to the stock. Mr. Marler don't cotton to neglectin' his cows. That cowboy is alright but he won't know about puttin' hay out for stock what roamed away. I'd appreciate your feedin' them mules and just leave them staked. There's plenty of wood and you'll be dry here. I'll return in a couple of days."

After the fire was built up, Amos settled beside it in his bedroll. He contemplated Senner's actions. Everyone calculated that the miner had about 1000 pounds of ore of the richest kind. Amos decided after having known the young man that he probably cobbed the ore first. He was a clever man that was ob-

Phoenix Daily Herald,
June 23, 1893,
P. 4, Col. 2.

Another gentleman arriving from up country this morning, reports the "Kid" as having been seen near the mouth of Tonto Creek, and that the engineers of the Hudson Reservoir Company are counting noses at the end of each day's work, lest a few [illegible] got escape.

vious. And, they talked about what it was worth but Senner had said it was near $250,000.00. It really didn't matter who was right—either one would be a king's ransom. Now that he was actually out here, Amos had new respect for Al Senner. He even hoped the young man had made it back, taken Katie, and was off having a wonderful life. What troubled him most was the statement Joe Gibson made about it being tough to mount the canyon pulling along the pack animals and still control your own. Al only had one arm but none of those people in Goldfield knew that.

Lunch was some warmed over beans, bread and coffee. The rain moved in steady now. The fire made lunch more bearable because it was getting mighty cold. Amos's thoughts went right back to Senner and the puzzle. He imagined there were about 12 ounces per pound to the gold. Gold was $20.60 per ounce, if Al had only 500 pounds that would be $110,000.00. . .The doctor grunted. Imagine finding a cache like that? He had inherited Mrs. Mason's home and furnishings; he had a thriving practice and he was becoming a prominent member of the town of Florence. In fact, wanting that gold seemed greedy but the very thought of finding it gave him a chill. He guessed this was what people meant when they talked about gold-fever.

On the second day about four o'clock Joe Gibson returned. Amos had to admit the sight of him was welcoming. Being in that cave for two days had definitely lost its charm.

The weather had cleared some. Joe said coming in from the ranch he could see that the top of Superstition Mountain was covered with snow. They agreed to start out early the next morning. Amos had trouble getting to sleep and had to admit to himself that he was giddy with anticipation.

Chapter 10

The Mesa

Joe bristled. The wind, tearing through the canyon, made starting a fire difficult and putting a back to it, the cowboy blew hard into the flame trying to ignite a few sticks of scrub. They both needed coffee and some hot grub to sustain them for the treacherous climb up the mountain. A good decision made the night before, to leave one of the mules hobbled near some grain and a running stream, was arrived at easily. At least, Joe decided, he was dealing with a reasonable man. The other mule was packed and ready to pull their equipment just in case they were forced to stay the night. And, since the weather had been completely unpredictable, their caution made perfect sense.

The doctor huddled into a poncho as they started out in a bitter cold wind which seemed to cut right through them. Joe led them toward a trail now obscured by the snow which took him quite a while to actually find. When he did, he motioned to the doctor to follow along. Now, they were on a steep slant moving slowly up the snow slick trail. They would snake their climb, treading cautiously as they rose above the canyon. Within an hour Amos glanced below with a start. It was almost straight down and they still had a long way to go. Amos's horse slipped. Suddenly, the wet shale gave way, sending the mare down on her knees. The doctor quickly jerked on the rein, lifting, nervously hoping the horse could rise up. She did. He sighed, grunting with relief. They curled higher—man and beast fully aware of their precarious situation. There was a grandeur about the view both in back of them, where Weaver's Needle rose some 1800 feet into the air, and the expanse off in the distance of desert and mountains. One could only imagine where Senner might have first come up here and if he really did salt his cache in this place. The musings were short lived as Amos heard an unusual sound which seemed to be growing louder.

Finally he yelled, "What is that sound?"

"Water. The snow is melting and we are going to run into some trouble up ahead."

Joe shook his head. It wasn't the first time he'd tried telling some dude how tough the Superstitions were. It seemed to the cowboy they never believed him. Showing someone was the only solution but that could often be dangerous; now, he hoped they would make it back to the cave without a mishap.

As they switch-backed toward the main body of the mountain, the pack mule slid on ice; went off the trail and rolled down 200 feet below them. He looked unhurt but his fear was evidenced by loud bleating. The fearful wailing affected their horses, who danced helplessly as if to tell the men it was not safe. Joe jumped from his mount and hurried back to the place where the mule fell. The animal was safely wedged into the side of a rock. Moving sideways, he made his way carefully down the wet slope to reach him, slipping off his feet often; falling; then, righting himself, all the while talking softly to the frightened animal. Eventually, he coaxed the mule onto his feet again and began to lead him up the side of the canyon back onto the narrow trail. Once up, Joe readjusted his load causing the mule to honk loudly in agreement. Then, Joe bent into the fierce wind; tugging on the animal's lead and mounted his horse.

They continued ever so slowly. The cowboy, more cautious than before, cared about his stock, and was determined not to see them hurt. They crossed a deep cut in the mountain—momentarily away from the sheer sides, dipping into deep snow in a small canyon and headed for an arroyo.

Amos's eyes bulged.

"This is usually dry, Doc. I guess it's pretty deep, so take it easy." Joe yelled over the roar.

Tumultuous water, pummeling shale and dirt, pulling rocks and boulders down the steep mountain made an unbelievable sound. Amos doubted if they could get across in one piece. He sure as hell didn't want to chance it. In an instant Joe entered the roaring terror pulling the struggling mule behind him. It seemed forever but it was only a minute until the cowboy pulled all of the gear up beside him on a flat snow covered mound on the far side. Praying seemed natural as Amos followed. When a man's instincts told him something was foolhardy he could refuse but the whole trip had been at his insistence. The water raced at them. The horse's obsidian eyes glistened as he raced for the other side in a panic. Just before they jumped to safety, a rock splashed out of the torrent and hit Amos in the neck. His hand flew to the cut. He yelled loud, rushing to the mound beside the mule. Joe handed the doctor a wipe from a saddle bag. Amos, still shaken, pulled the fabric around the cut and tied it off.

"You okay, Doc?"

The doctor's face appeared chalky. He was still in shock from the near tragedy and his hand shook noticeably. He glanced back at the water. If they had gone down they both would have been dead by now—drowned or worse. All of his bravado diminished in the face of certain death. The mare, loyal and responsive, still fidgeted, Amos loosened the reins allowing her her head. Now, they were wet and the cold wind seemed to freeze everything immediately. Amos got down and wiped the horse's coat dry, speaking confidently to the mare as he rubbed. Mounting her, he reached back and patted her coat, saying in a loud voice.

"Good girl, let's go."

Joe moved on ahead calling back, "Don't fret, Doc, just one

more and we are on top."

The wind, increasing by the minute, seemed to scream. Amos snuggled down into his poncho pulling his ten gallon tight over his skull before tying the muffler around his mouth and nose and spread the big poncho over the mare's flank.

They dipped into another canyon. The arroyo raged off the mesa with unbelievable force and seemed to swirl as it rounded a curve near where they stood. Joe decided they would be better off crossing just above the bend. He climbed into the water, clutching the mule's rope and tied it quickly around the saddle horn. The mule honked loudly; remembering its recent terrifying experience; his shod-feet searched for solid ground and not finding it, moved ahead quicker than Joe's horse. It was uncomfortable to watch. Amos actually sweated until they were across. Once on the other side, Joe threw a lasso across to Amos who grabbed it and tied it to the horn. Joe worked his horse backwards until the doctor came into the river and started to move towards them. The stallion, an experienced cutter, backed further pulling the rope taut. Amos moved on, his stomach knotted with fear. It was the same terror he'd felt before, only this time they were anchored to the stallion and mule. What turned out to be five minutes seemed forever. Finally, his mare leaped up onto the far bank and raced away from the torrent. The doctor actually topped out on Superstition Mesa within minutes, he yelled and danced his horse around in circles. . .yelling Ya-Ha. . .Ya-Ha. . .and laughing as the mare reared with joy.

The snow was a foot deep on top. They were in blinding sunlight reflecting on the pure white snow but from their vantage point they could see Mesa City and Phoenix off in the distance. Behind them, rising up in all its raw beauty was Weaver's Needle, the peak so well known in the territory, which seemed spectacular from this vantage point. Amos stood just staring at it. He was cold and tired, a victim of the piercing wind racing across the mesa and yet, he couldn't resist being in awe at the grandeur which seemed close enough to touch.

Goldfield Pond *Credit: Salt River Project History Services*

Joe had gone on ahead. There wasn't anything in these mountains he hadn't seen before. He didn't like the job he was doing but he figured with 5 ten dollar gold pieces in his chaps, he'd have a lot better chance of getting that new horse at the Phoenix auction.

The wind was shrill. It had driven deep drifts along the hillsides and pinyons. Blowing powder irritating their eyes forced Amos to squint in order to see the dangerous trail they had covered. Joe had pulled his wipes over his mouth and nose and used a second one to tie down his ten gallon. Amos looked ominous with the muffler covering his hat, face and chin. A huge grunt erupted while he swiped at his forehead with a sleeve. It had taken five hours but they were on top and it felt good to have achieved it.

For the next hour they made their way along the northwestern edge of Superstition Mountain. Eventually, leaving the ridge-back, they picked their way into a boulder strewn valley. Joe pointed up ahead. The horses shied occasionally as they skirted snow covered rocks while moving cautiously over the rough terrain. Joe spotted a lean-to near a boulder patch. It was the first sign of life anywhere but it looked crude and forlorn. They rode toward it and dismounted. Someone had camped there recently. They dug into the snow and found some personal belongings: a comb, a razor, a canteen full of ice, and cooking utensils. Whoever had camped there expected to return, but the camp looked as if it hadn't been used for several weeks. Joe tramped away from the lean-to looking for clues. Amos knelt by a mound in the snow next to a small pinyon tree. His gloved hand pulled up a single shot 45-70 trap-door rifle with a cartridge in the chamber. He brushed the snow from the stock, shaking the gun to clear the snow from the barrel and held it up to look at it. Next to it, under five inches of new snow, he found another frozen canteen. He stood glancing around and thinking that something had surely happened to the man who lived in this camp.

Joe called to Amos. He hurried across the snow to a clump of boulders near a hill where the cowboy was scraping snow off a carcass.

"It's a mule. He was tied to a stake and probably died of starvation or thirst. Whoever was camped here very definitely meant to return but I don't think they ever did."

Joe pulled his wipes off his nose; the sunbronzed face stared up at the doctor. "Do you recognize any of this stuff, Doc?"

"No, but I think we need to look further."

By now Amos was convinced he had found Senner's camp and a real sadness was overtaking him. Standing, and glancing around the site, he hurried toward the lean-to and went inside. The snow hadn't penetrated the canvas; it was dark and the meager contents wrapped in hoar frost laid near the charred remnants of a long dead fire. Stooping, Amos examined a bedcover and blanket under which he found a black leather bag. It was small and badly worn but which contained a treasure. Shaking from cold, the big man pulled at his glove with his teeth; then, stiff fingers reached into the leather. He extracted a picture of a beautiful young woman. She had a bright smile and her eyes seemed to sparkle. On the bottom in very precise writing it was signed, "To Al With Love, Katie." Amos swore. Also in the bag, tied with string, was a packet of letters addressed to Al Senner, Goldfield, Arizona. The one on top bore a date of October 17, 1893.

The doctor yelled to Joe and came out into the sunlight. "I found evidence, Joe, here, see!"

The cowboy hurried toward him.

Joe was stoic. He suspected that the man was dead...had met with foul play or an accident. Whatever the reason, they had just made a very dangerous climb to find out.

Without wasting a moment, he said, "We ought to start down, Doc. It won't take us long but I wouldn't want to attempt that trail in the dark especially in this cold and with the wind blowing. That newly melted snow will be ice by dark."

"I'd like to stay the night, Joe. I mean, if he is up here, maybe we can find the body, or at least, discover what happened. Will you do it?" His eyes searched the cowboy's face hoping for acceptance. Joe pulled off his hat and scratched his head, an old habit. It took only a few seconds and then, without a word, he went directly to the pack mule and began to unload.

"Doc," he called from the animal's side. "You'd better get equipped. It's gonna be colder than hell up here tonight. I expect we'd better shore up that lean-to and get the animals in somewhere protected.

Amos climbed onto his horse. The wind was still howling but he didn't seem to mind. Part of the puzzle had been solved. The fact that Senner hadn't cheated him renewed his faith in his fellow man. Amos wasn't soft: he had been a soldier, worked in the mines tending really damaged men, built a practice, and had traveled half way across the United States alone; but he believed in people and wanted to continue to do that. It seemed so strange to him that Al Senner had survived that horrible beating and the delirium that followed, roamed in the desert half dead, had his arm amputated and lived, just to come here to die. He was driven to know what had happened. It seemed pretty likely that Senner was dead and Amos was feeling a grief of sorts.

The snow blinded rider and horse. They didn't roam far. In a boulder clump, near the lean-to, he found a spot for the animals. He got off and tethered the mare before he put the poncho over her and tied it around her neck and back. He led her inside and gave her some hay. Joe brought the mule. He stopped to allow the animal a drink from a rock pool nearby. They had both drank their fill at the arroyo—at least, they wouldn't have that problem.

Soon, they brought the blankets and tarps inside and built a fire. Joe busied himself outside tying the boards with a lasso and piling rocks up against them. He carried wood inside and stacked it. There wouldn't be much room, but at least they would be out of the wind.

Shortly, a fire crackled loudly in the small enclosure. The coffee pot boiled in the flames blackening the sides. Amos put out their tin cups in anticipation, smiling eagerly. He laid a pot beside the coffee pot and scooped beans from a can into it. There was stew in a tin and some bread left from yesterday, which had hardened, but which might be tasty sopping up the juice from the stew. Both men were starving by the time they ate.

Outside a gale blew against them. The temperature dropped quickly and Joe's eyes evidenced his concern.

"We'd better take turns staying awake to keep this fire going, Doc. It's going to snow again and this time we are goin' to be near enough to hell to smell smoke."

After the food staying awake wasn't easy. They'd had a hard day. That night it sleeted along with screaming wind and new snow. They bundled into their sleeping tarps and each man took turns tending to the fire; it was the difference between life and death. Near dawn the storm subsided. Joe peered out at the foot of fresh snow piled on top of the mesa. The temperature was bitter at dawn but by nine the sun began to warm them and, eventually, melted most of the snow. It was, however, now wet and slick and the low temperatures produced ice.

"We'll have to stay another day," Joe announced as they rode across the face of the big mesa. "This ground is too slippery. We'd never get down alive."

Amos groaned. He had new respect for Joe and for the place. 'No wonder Senner put his gold up here,' he thought. 'Not many men would scale that trail to get up here.'

As they rode around the edge of the mountain Joe speculated that Senner must have rode his horse off of one of the cliffs. Both of them agreed Senner planned to return or he wouldn't have left the animal staked and the gun by his digs.

There was a long twelve hour night ahead of them. The storm passed but the temperatures continued down. Fortunately, there was sufficient wood and they were diligent about keeping the flames up. At ten the next day, most of the snow had melted leaving ice in its wake. They saddled their animals to begin a systematic search of the mountain top. On the southwestern end by the edge of the cliff they found a spot where the trail passed dangerously close to the edge and it looked as if the earth had given way recently. Dismounting, the doctor knelt down and crawled close to allow him a clear view of the chasm below. It was at least 800 feet to a boulder strewn canyon. Gibson, waiting nearby, issued a caution.

Down below, barely discernable, were the carcasses of two dead animals lying near each other. Amos called to Joe to verify what he saw.

"Joe, I'm going to climb down there. I know that it'll solve the mystery once and for all."

The cowboy offered to stay at the site and direct the doctor from the vantage point just above. It seemed reasonable, and they both agreed. Then, taking his lasso, Joe secured it to a rock and threw it over the side at the place where Amos was about to descend.

Chapter 11

The Whole Story

Lowering himself over the edge was frightening; Amos hadn't relished the thought of the long climb down to what looked like a disaster. It was at least 800 feet. Under the precipice wasn't sheer but extremely steep. There were boulders and rocks which he might be able to grab a hold of as he moved and the rope would only help for a short distance, but then, he would be on his own. Since there was no trail, he couldn't plan ahead. The boots were not effective on rock and the earth was still wet from the recent storms. No one would have attempted the climb without his particular motivation and there were times during it when he seriously doubted the wisdom of his decision. He was, however, already committed.

Joe called from above often. It was reassuring to hear a human voice. The doctor's hands were now bleeding; he had barely noticed but finally, realizing it was cold, he remembered his gloves and put them on. At one point he knew he would have to jump or slip across the sheer rock just below with almost no toe-hold. The pointed toes on his boots aided digging into the basalt crevice, but it was dangerous, and if he fell there was not much chance that he would survive it without broken bones. A sweat raised on Amos' upper lip which caused him to pause briefly and cautiously glance up at the place where, he believed, Senner fell. After crossing the rock face, Amos looked down.

It seemed he had gone about half way and although that was somewhat satisfying, the rest of the climb didn't appear to be too easy to accomplish. After coming to a flat spot flanked by two good sized rocks, he sat down to rest. From this vantage point he could see out to the distant valley and mountains but his view of the accident site was obscured.

Mesa City was in plain sight. Amos shuddered at the thought of falling from this height to the valley floor below. He had consciously avoided allowing himself to see where the mountain ended. Instead, he made certain calculations about the rest of the journey and what would ultimately happen to the information. Then, he began to wonder if the gold was laying in the canyon under Senner's body. It also occurred to him the dead animals might be covering it. Whatever the case, he knew the sight and smells awaiting him would not be pretty. Senner had now been dead for several months. The winter storms and cold nights at this altitude would help, but, he wondered, 'are the vultures yet to come or have they already been here?'

A half an hour later Amos's feet touched the bottom of the small canyon. He sighed heavily, looked up and waved to Joe who was hanging over the precipice's edge. Just 100 feet to the east he saw the torn carcasses of the horse and mule. "My God," he said aloud. "I have never seen anything like it." The animals were so badly mangled and the stench of their decaying bodies was even more disgusting than he had imagined. Not being one to avoid a problem, Amos moved to the sight and quickly tied his handkerchief around his nose and mouth. The actual scene of the accident left him overwhelmed.

Senner was unrecognizable. Amos moved some rocks and searched for the dead man's arms. Eventually, he saw what had been his own work; the left arm amputated just below the elbow. Upon further examination, he saw a folded paper sticking out of a pocket which he quickly removed. Moving away from the appalling scene, Amos opened it. He sat down. It was a map of the mesa giving exact directions to Al's camp and the treasure with his signature, the date and remarks about Katie. In essence it was a will. Amos looked up at the sky; it was bright blue. 'Strange,' he thought, 'Here I am looking at the will of a man I befriended who came to his untimely end in this God forsaken place. He wanted so to have a good life with this woman. He must have decided to leave her the money just in case she didn't want to live with a maimed husband. Or maybe, he had decided not to go back to her. . .after all of this.' The doctor shook his head. 'What a powerful story with such a tragic ending.'

It all seemed unreal. Amos walked away from the sight a good distance and took a deep breath. Looking back, he decided that Al Senner deserved a grave. There was a spot where he could actually dump the body and cover it with rocks. 'I owe you that,' he thought before grimacing to prepare for the grotesque task.

There were some trees laying nearby in an arroyo filled with melting snow. Amos gathered them to wedge beneath the body. Once they were in place, he pushed and tugged until he could actually shove the decaying form into a shallow grave just under a large rock formation. It didn't take long to gather rocks and begin to put them over Senner. Finally, when his work was completed, Amos Basset removed his ten gallon hat, bowed his head and spoke the words her felt Senner would have wanted.

"God, this is Amos Basset. I came here to find a young man whom I befriended. I believed in him. You've got him now and I'm glad I know what happened here. I am sorry for that young woman who loves him so. I don't know what I might do about that but it rests my mind to know about Al. It's late I know, but please, look after this soul. Amen."

That having been taken care of Amos thought about the gold. And, as unpleasant a chore as it was, he did examine the panniers on the horse. There was no doubt that the gold had been transferred in that leather. Some of it adhered to the inside seam. Amos scooped it out. There were a few nuggets, very small, and some dust. He examined the area thoroughly. Gazing up where he could see Joe Gibson, he calculated how the fall occurred. But, even retracing all of the movement, he could not find any gold. Amos sat down on a distant rock to rethink his position. 'Maybe, the animals lost the gold as they tumbled into the air.' That thought drew him to other spots in the canyon where he carefully scratched the surface of the earth and moved limbs and soft mud. He was in that place for a long time but to no avail.

Joe called down to him to return. Amos agreed.

The climb back up was equally dangerous but it didn't seem to matter. Finally, Joe's big hand stretched above him in the air and as he accepted it, he knew he was safe. Being pulled onto the mesa by strong hands gave him real satisfaction. The pair stared at each other. Joe said, "Well, Doc, guess you found out what we come here for?"

"Yes. I did. At least I can rest easy that the man told me the truth. I hate the fact that he is dead, but now, I can stop speculating about it."

Joe grinned before removing the big hat. "Did you bury him? Is that what was takin' you so long?"

The doctor nodded.

They both agreed Al Senner was probably riding along the edge of the mesa, pulling the mule behind him, when the earth must have given away. Amos visualized that scene and grimaced. In his mind he could hear the man's screams and the panicked sound of the animals who were careening to certain death. He glanced away in the direction of the grave down below and felt deep sadness.

"Well, at least, they died instantly. No one survived that fall. I think that was the only kindness the Lord allowed."

Joe nodded and mounted his horse. "I figure we ought to break camp, Doc. We still got a long trip and the day is gettin' on."

The packing didn't take long after they returned to Senner's camp.

Amos collected the rifle, headed toward the horse and slid

the gun into the bedroll behind his saddle. The leather pouch, containing Katie's photograph and letters, was put into his saddle bag. There wasn't any denying that he was curious as to what she'd said, but, for the moment, he wasn't going to consider whether he would read them or not.

After the mule was loaded, Joe mounted his stallion for the trip off the mesa. The sun hung bright over them and it had warmed up considerably. Amos pulled the brim of his hat down to shield his eyes from its rays. He waited for Joe to lead the mule off, then followed along slowly. At the ridge he paused and glanced back, Senner's crude lean-to sat nakedly in the breeze. Amos knew he would never forget this place.

They started down around noon. The trail continued to be muddy and slick. It gave them pause as they carefully led their animals over rocks and shale which shifted easily when it was trod upon. The arroyos were slowing. Amos grinned when he saw them. No man would opt to cross that tumult a second time.

He stopped just short of the turn in the trail to have a last look at the view from the summit. There were no words to describe the beauty just out from the mesa. He imagined Senner looking out from this place and even wondered if the miner had been sensitive to the extraordinary landscape. It was rough. Great rock formations piled high, spearing into a cornflower blue sky bright with sunlight. It appeared that the range was untouchable—a place where man and beast were unwelcome but which beckoned mysteriously. The fates had salted gold and silver into this place and the knowledge of it plagued men's souls causing them to do murderous things. Had Senner been the thief and con man he was accused of being? Amos figured he would probably never know, but, at least he had allowed himself the discovery, and now, he knew what had happened to his patient. There was some comfort in that knowledge. It was expedient not to tell Joe Gibson the real reason for the trip to the top of hell. And, he was glad he didn't mention the amputation; in fact, no one knew the true story except Amos Basset, and for

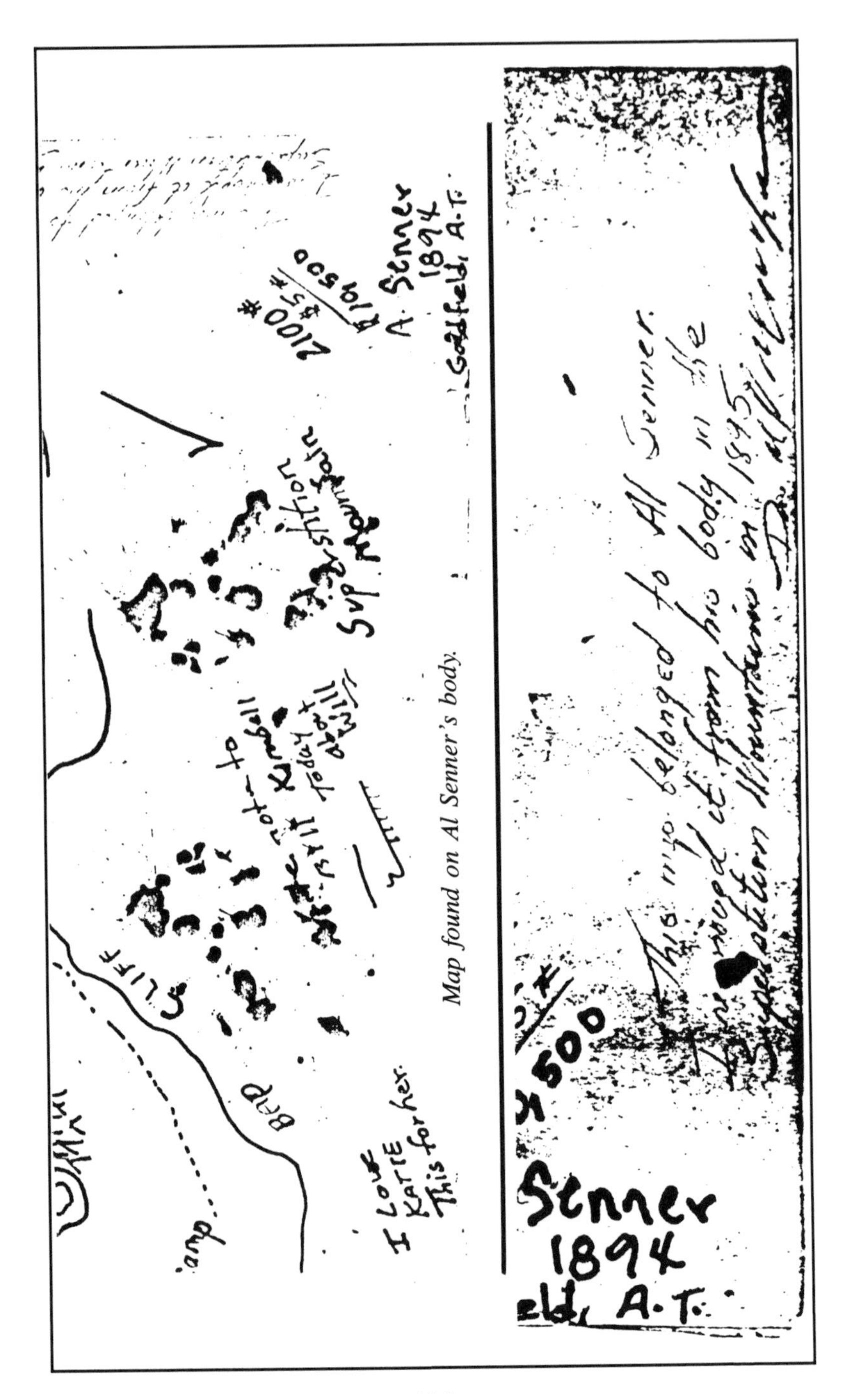

Map found on Al Senner's body.

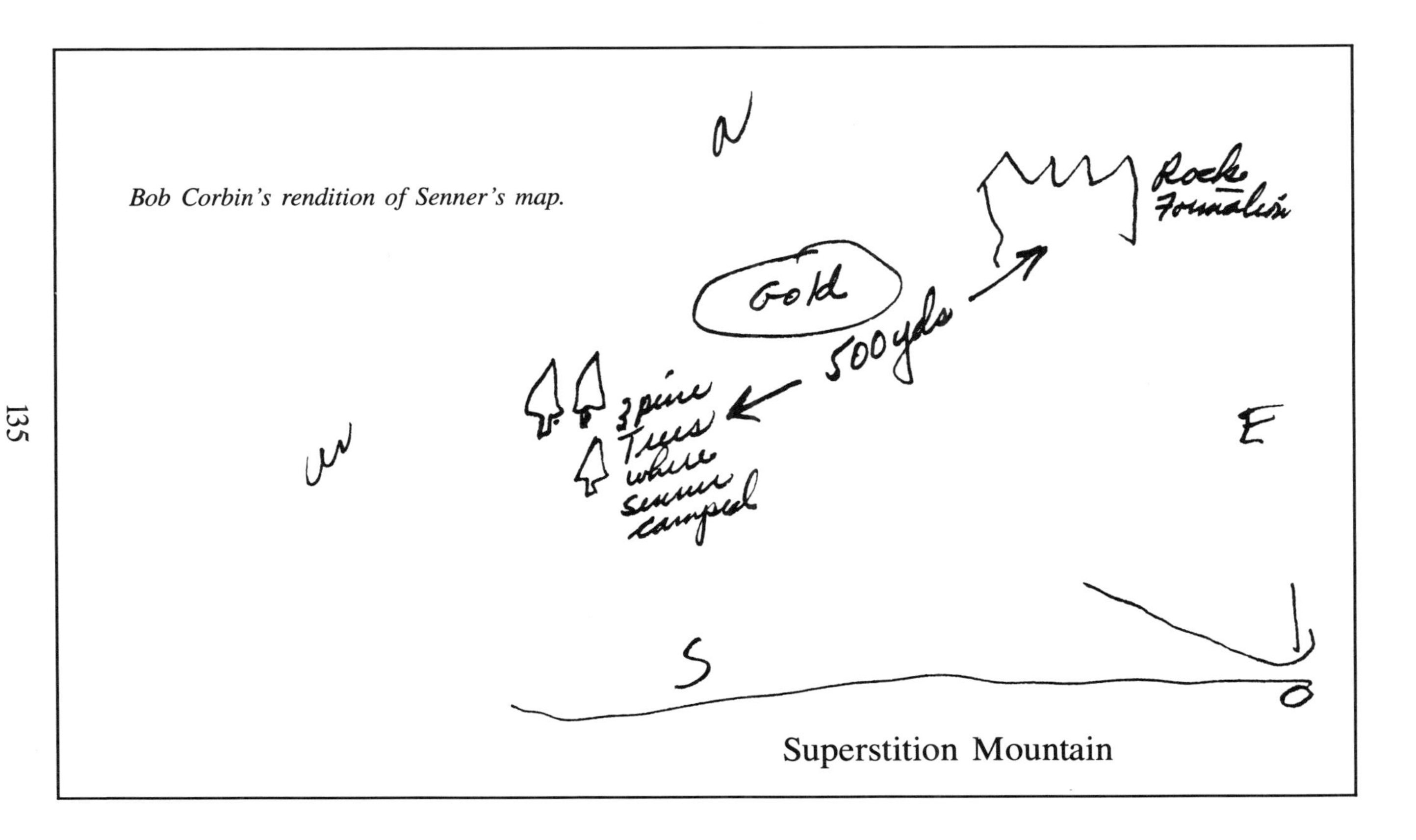

Bob Corbin's rendition of Senner's map.

now, no one would know. As he sat there in a creaking saddle he wondered if he would come back here again and hunt for Senner's lost gold?

The cowboy's voice jolted his being. "Come on, Doc, it's getting late. It'll take three hours to make it down the trail."

A loud snort proceeded the mare's uneven descent. They were equally glad to be leaving this place. Amos leaned back in the saddle, helping her as best he could as she picked her way along the steep, rocky path. It was over a thousand feet down and the animals knew what was in store for them if they slipped. Out beyond the trail lay a great canyon bordered by sheer rock walls and cut in the middle with a rocky stream. It couldn't have been more beautiful or more treacherous.

The sun was just slipping below the western edge of the mesa when Joe called to halt.

"We're down, Doc, and I for one am glad," he yelled into the canyon. His voice echoed back.

Amos grinned at the cowboy's words. He was not alone—it had been a tough trip and he was glad it was almost over. It seemed welcoming to hear the hoof beats on wet rocks as they made their way along the canyon floor toward the cave. The hobbled mule heard them coming and began to honk a greeting. Both men knew the animal was glad to hear them return. He must have been wondering if he had been abandoned. That moment allowed Amos a thought about the mule Senner had left staked to the tree on the mesa. He must have waited for those sounds too but they never came.

They dismounted and unsaddled their horses. It was shadowy at dusk, deep in the canyon, but not yet dark. Amos hurried to build a fire.

Joe busied himself preparing their meal. Tonight they would feast on some beef and beans with coffee and good homemade biscuits, which were a source of pride. The bottle was in his saddle bags; he hurried to retrieve it and after he returned, pulled out the cork with his teeth and offered Amos a swig.

The whiskey tasted good. Amos took a pull and handed it back, smirking as he did. "I'll bet you never thought we'd be celebrating tonight—did you?"

Joe grinned. "Well, Doc, you never know about a guy. I'm just glad you found out what happened to your friend. It's rotten to go on a wonderin'. Did he have family?"

"I don't think so, Joe, but there was the girl in Mesa City. She will take it real hard, I'll bet."

Joe moved toward the fire to begin cooking. The sounds were reassuring to the doctor as he fed the animals outside in their makeshift corral. Shortly, carrying his saddle and blanket, he returned to the inside of the cave and laid them on the edge of his sleeping tarp. He flopped down with a grunt, leaned heavily against leather and complained that he was both tired and hungry. Joe laughed before telling him the grub would be ready shortly; then, he dropped what was left of their bacon into the skillet with the beef.

"I don't mind telling you, Joe, that bacon smells better than anything I ever smelled." The pungent aroma filled the cave. Amos inhaled it and grinned, laying back to watch the smoke lifting to the high slanted rock ceiling above them.

Joe knew what his client was feeling. They had been in the saddle all day traveling over dangerous terrain. The excitement alone would have created an appetite, but, they had climbed and worked since sun-up. The cook felt the same way and busied himself turning the meat which sizzled in the black pan. A big iron pot full of biscuits sat in the flames. They'd have fresh hot biscuits with their coffee and Joe's homemade prickly pear jam which was always welcomed at any camp meal. It was a quiet meal; they both chewed with vigor. Later, the full moon rose high over the mesa. It cast its shadows down tall canyon walls and lit a path over the water where the mules and horses rested. A coyote wailed its lonely call into the silence of the night. The only other sounds were the crackling embers of a dying fire and the snores of two contented riders.

The morning dawned bright. Joe was already up and busying himself over breakfast. They were both eager to head for the ranch. They talked about the trip back while they ate the beans and left over biscuits from the night before. Amos poured some more coffee while Joe went to unhobble the mule. He hurried to release her and laughed at the animal's honking approval. The cowboy's experienced hands leveled the load and tied it into place. He gave her some grain as a reward.

* * *

The ranch sat up against the base of Superstition Mountain enjoying its shadow at certain times of the day. They had moved carefully through the brush and crossed a curling creek flush with winter run off. Amos particularly liked the sounds of the hoof beats in the water and over wet rocks as they moved along. It was almost dusk when they caught sight of the buildings and came into the corral past the long trail of palo verde trees.

By dark the men sat enjoying a campfire. A full moon rose above the ranch, lighting the area and allowing a good view of the mountain beyond. Amos stared up at it. Then, he got up and went over to Joe who was fixing them both some coffee.

"Joe, I've added another twenty to the fee." He stretched out his open palm toward the cowboy. "It doesn't seem like half enough after what you did for me. You see, I really liked that young man. I feel bad that he's dead but not knowing was driving me crazy. I wouldn't have wanted to live my whole life not knowing. If it hadn't been for your generosity, I might never have known. I don't know of any other man who would have taken me up that mountain and I don't think I could have survived it alone. It was very dangerous. In fact, there were times when I regretted my decision but you just pushed on without any seeming fear. Thanks."

The cowboy accepted the gold pieces without a word. Neither of them needed any more discussion. It was over and settled.

Joe didn't want to get involved with death certificates and such. Amos had never discussed the amputation or Goldfield. No one else knew where Amos had gone. There would be no discussion about it and Al Senner's name had never come up. If Amos chose to return at some later date, he alone would be privy to the secret.

* * *

The trip home was made the following day. As Amos neared the road to Florence, he decided to stop at the Sheriff's office and file a death certificate and certify it. He was the attending physician. It seemed the proper thing to do.

It was dusk and the town was very quiet. The Sheriff's Office was empty except for one deputy who had just returned from the hotel where he had enjoyed a particularly good dinner. The toothpick in the side of his plump lips attested to that fact. Amos waited patiently for the man to look up from the desk where he seemed preoccupied with a letter.

"Oh, it's you, Doc. Sorry, I didn't see you there." The man got up and walked toward the counter.

"It's just fine. I recently returned from the Superstitions where I found Al Senner's body—he was killed in a fall from a mountain—been dead about two months. I filed a missing persons report earlier—we need to cancel that and I'll fill out a death certificate. Have you got one handy?"

The deputy returned with the necessary paper-work and handed it to the doctor. He scratched away with a quill pen and signed it. The officer pulled out a stamp and made it official. They grinned knowingly at each other. Amos nodded, pulled at the brim of his ten gallon and turned toward the door. He mounted the mare, heaved a huge sigh and turned the lead toward his home, relishing the fact that he would be spending the night in his big feathered bed.

As Amos rode into the side yard, he warmed to the welcoming oil lamp sending lemon shafts of light into the garden. After dismounting, he led the mare toward the barn and immediately lit the lamp. He spoke softly to the animal, telling her how glad they both were to be home. Lifting the saddle and hoisting it onto the rack, he pulled the mare to the stall and watched, grinning, as she grabbed a mouthful of hay. Amos wiped her down quickly. He was tired and he wanted to get into bed.

Inside, the doctor headed for his study where the lamp was already lit. The mail lying on the desk called to him. He thought of ignoring it; he was too tired, but before he turned away, a postmark caught his eye. It looked like Los Angeles. Pulling off the ten gallon, Amos threw it onto the couch then sat down and opened the letter.

March 10, 1895

Dear Doctor Basset,

I'm certain that my letter will come as a surprise but I hope it will be wecome. You and I have been corresponding for some years now, and I have always felt that you would make an excellent choice for a future partner. Your interest in my surgical techniques allowed me to feel that with the proper training you could become a very fine surgeon.

Naturally, I would expect you to take the proper time to cancel your practice and sell your home if you are interested. I am however in great need of an assistant as my practice is growing entirely too fast.

Please advise me as to your decision as soon as possible.

Very truly yours,
Doctor Marcus Wellman

The big man sat back in his swivel and leaned his head to

one side. It was all too much. First, there was this business with the gold. . .then, Senner's death and now, . . .wonder of all wonders, a position with the finest surgeon in the West. He laughed out loud. "God. . .Life is really strange."

He stood up. He was bone tired when he entered the room and now, without thought, he had more energy than he would have believed possible. It seemed extraordinary but he was going to Los Angeles to start a new life.

Chapter 12

Katie's Destiny

It took several years for Mesa City to forget about Senner. Katie's once exuberant smile faded into stoic remorse. It wasn't anything tangible. People often ignore the troubles of others; rarely noticing the subtle changes which later become their norm. Folks still referred to her as beautiful but it was in passing or an offhand remark. And, there were other matters of greater importance which occupied everyone.

Bill Kimball hurried into his office at the hotel. He was expecting an important letter. Not finding it, the man quickly approached his desk clerk. "Are you certain I didn't get a letter from Denver?" he demanded.

"No, Sir." The clerk paled as he spoke. "I did just like you asked, Mr. Kimball. I went to the post office and came straight here with all of the mail. It is on your desk." He pointed toward the office looking frustrated.

The big man mumbled something inaudible, turned on his heel and using determined strides, moved into his office. The clerk scrinched up his shoulders and squinted, awaiting the sound of the slammed door. When it came, he relaxed and heaved a huge sigh.

Katie came down the staircase. "Good morning, George. You don't look very well. Is there something wrong?"

A desk clerk shuffled some papers before whispering, "Mam,

it's the boss—he's real mad. I didn't do anything and he... well...I just don't know. It ain't like him."

Softening a smile, Katie said, "Don't take it to heart, George. Mr. Kimball has a lot of problems right now. He probably doesn't even know that you are afraid." Her businesslike manner returned. She turned and walked swiftly into the dining room before entering the long kitchen.

The Chinese cook looked up and grinned. There was a special bond between Katie and Cholly, not much conversation but an empathy of sorts and an unspoken understanding. "You leady for lunch, Mliss Katie?"

"No, Cholly. I'm really not. I don't know what is wrong with me today. It is as if I'm dragging a big rock on a rope around my leg. It is an effort to do anything. I'm certain it's the result of all this trouble with Goldfield closing. Mr. Kimball is having real financial problems. He shipped all of the goods the store owners asked for on credit and now, they have disappeared."

"You tink dey not pay?" His eyes grew wide and concerned.

"Yes, Cholly, I do. Mr. Kimball has a lot of expenses with the freight and stage line. He bought all of those new coachs and now they aren't being used."

The cook's black pigtail flipped sideways as he shook his head. "Me no understand, Mliss Katie. Why do people wolly so mluch?"

The statement raised a smile. "Oh, Cholly, you are so dear. I don't know what I would do without you." She came close and hugged him lightly.

Cholly flushed under his yellow skin, then he hurried back to the stove and began to stir the soup. The steam raised in large puffs engulfing Cholly, who disappeared behind the stoves. Lunch was almost ready.

Exiting the kitchen, Katie went to the desk. "George, if Mr. Kimball wants me, please tell him I've gone to the mercantile. I'll be back before the lunch crowd comes in."

The young clerk nodded and watched her leave.

It was sunny. The winds of March were slowing and the temperature was just right. Katie had every reason to be happy. For a change she felt eager to do something and making this decision had been difficult. For years, ever since she lost her man, Katie lived in an emotional limbo. Even today going to the mercantile to discuss the matter plagued her. The resolve came just at the moment the clerk confessed how angry her boss was. Kimball had talked of selling the hotel. She didn't want to work for anyone else. Kimball House had been her home ever since she arrived in Mesa City. A slim smile crossed the full lips. Then, remembering those first days, she actually laughed. She was a green as grass—broke but free.

Leaving home at 18 with almost no money and no way to get back, took real courage. Katie felt fortunate to have met Bill Kimball that first day after climbing off the stage coach in Mesa City. The plan was to go to Phoenix, but the stage didn't stop there. This was as far as saved money would allow. The owner was eating lunch in the boardinghouse dining room; he watched her silently for a long time, got up and approached her. He was kind, making Katie feel welcome, then, offered a job and a place to stay. Kimball was more than patient every step of the way. There were never any unkind words over broken plates or mixed up orders. In time it paid off. Katie, who had never worked before, turned out to be Bill Kimball's right arm. When the hotel was enlarged, the dining room was designed under her direction. She had strength of character and common sense. Kimball told everyone what a capable, decent woman she was. And no one could have been more sympathetic after Senner disappeared. In fact, he used all of his influence to learn everything he could about the incident. He believed, as did everyone else, Al Senner was a highgrader and a thief but he said as little as possible to Katie, whom he truly admired.

The businessman had a lot of claims at Goldfield. He also owned a bar and a boardinghouse; they all closed months ago. In fact, Goldfield's streets, now deserted, were claimed by the

March winds. The hotel owner had ridden there for one last look. It was as if only ghosts owned it. The powdered caliche blew across the desert smothering its empty buildings. Looking up, he saw the smelter, its stacks dormant, towering over the lonely scene. It was true—Goldfield was dead and all of his investments had gone down with it. He could kiss the money they owed him goodby. Feeling desolate, he jerked on the lead, turning his horse towards Mesa City.

After lunch Katie went up to her room. The decision to try to open her own shop weighed heavily. Sitting by the window, the young woman examined the money in the tin box. It was only $100.00. The owner of the mercantile liked her idea of purchasing cloth by the bolt for Katie's would be customers. Everyone knew she was a good seamstress. It wouldn't take long to build a clientele. In the meantime she would still work at Kimball House but only during dinner hours. Of course, as yet, Bill was unaware. He wasn't going to be happy about it. The new waitresses were doing well; he wasn't going to be left without help. Katie nodded. Accepting the fact she was being fair, the woman stood and faced the mirror. It was time to go to talk to him—no matter how unpleasant—it had to be done. Christmas had come and gone. . .they were actually into the third month of the new decade. It was 1900—high time she changed her life.

Kimball usually took lunch in his office. He was a particular man with a great intensity which was more than obvious to most people. The hotel was his main concern and now, that he had lost everything else, he was trying desperately to find a way to pay his bills. Goldfield had provided all manner of business both on the stage and freight lines and in his hotel and restaurant. Now, that was gone. He owned a lot to his wife who patiently accepted all of the trouble. There were four children to consider and the future looked bleak. Rising, Kimball paced in his large office. 'There might be someone in Phoenix who would buy the hotel,' he thought. The letters to Phoenix bankers and lenders had been sent. Maybe, it was time to ride over there for a chat. Having considered every other option, he picked up his hat and his briefcase containing the hotel's records, then hurried out.

Using the back stairwell, Katie entered the kitchen. Lunch was over, Cholly had cleaned up and gone to his quarters. Katie always marveled at Cholly's efficiency—the kitchen was immaculate. She pushed open the dining room door and started into the lobby just as the desk clerk entered.

"Oh! Miss Katie, Mr. Kimball gave me a message for you."

The woman stopped and looked expectant. "You mean he isn't here?" She seemed surprised.

"No mam. He went to Phoenix. He said to tell you he'd be back tomorrow. He wanted you to take over in the dining room."

Katie looked pensive. "Hmm. Okay, George—thank you."

Disappointed, Katie returned to the kitchen to make a cup of tea. This wasn't going to be easy and prolonging it only made it worse.

* * *

The dinner crowd filed into the dining room starting at 5 P.M. There were three waitresses, who waited in fresh white aprons and caps. Katie trained them all. A smile and good service was her motto. It worked. The dining room was a success, especially with Cholly's help. The Chinaman's food, well known as far away as Phoenix and Roosevelt Dam, caused comments every day. It was a source of pride to Kimball as well as the town.

At ten P.M., they closed the dining room. Katie felt relief. All night she had been feeling apprehension—as if there was something ominous happening. The staff was leaving. They each said goodnight. Cholly saved her some stew and a piece of apple pie. Katie liked to join him after everyone was gone. She went into the kitchen and sat down at the pie table. It was already set for two. The cook brought two steaming plates of stew and some homemade rolls. He went back to the ice-box for butter.

Katie put a napkin into her lap, watching her pleasant friend hurrying back to their dinner.

"It looks delicious, Cholly. I'm hungry too."

Cholly sat down. "Me rike stew too."

They began to eat and it was quiet.

"You sad, Mliss Katie?"

The woman looked up; her chewing slowed. "No. I feel troubled but I can't explain it. It is as though something bad is about to happen." She smiled across in an embarrassed way. "I guess I sound silly, don't I?"

"No, Mlissy. You wolly? Sometime, someting tell you."

The woman smiled across at him. He was actually her closest friend in town. Katie's independence prohibited asking for help when Senner disappeared, people were cruel. The Chinese cook had been the object of prejudice, he knew her pain but he also genuinely liked her.

Cholly came into the country as a young boy—slave labor for the railroads. He was sold to some ruthless Englishmen in his native land, then shipped by boat to San Francisco. Life had been ugly. He really appreciated his life in Mesa City and gave great loyalty to Kimball and Katie.

Katie remembered asking once to hear about his life. He began with the railroad gangs. When the roadbed West was completed, he wound up in Tombstone working as a clean up boy in a brothel named the Birdcage Saloon. That town turned wild—people were killed nightly and Cholly fled for his life. He jobbed anywhere he could for a long time and finally, met Bill Kimball, who asked him if he wanted to learn to cook. The young man was industrious, as were all of the orientals who came into the West. They never wound up on the dole or in trouble. Instead, they plowed along, learning everything they could and becoming proficient at many things. Naturally, they were penurious about money.

Katie watched Cholly sopping up the stew gravy with his bread and smacking his lips as he concluded. The joy with which the

Kimball House, which burned to the ground in 1900.
Photo courtesy of Charles Crismon, Director,
Farm and Heritage Museum in Mesa, Arizona.

man lived always encouraged her. He had taught the young woman a valuable lesson: if you didn't expect too much, life was much easier to accept.

Within a half an hour they finished. Katie excused herself to check the dining room to make certain it was all prepared for breakfast. After that she went upstairs to her room and prepared for bed. 'Bill will be back tomorrow and then I'll tell him my plan,' she thought. She was really tired, laid back and fell into a deep sleep.

It was two A.M. when the alarm sounded—a fire bell near the kitchen clanged loud, being sounded by a frightened cook. Everyone ran out into the corridors which were already smoke filled. Katie screamed for the guests to hurry out into the street. People filed down the big staircase in a panic. After making certain they were all out, Katie followed, but not before running back into the building to go to her room. A strong hand restrained her. It was a fireman from town. "No mam. You can't go in there—that place is an inferno. It's not safe."

"Please. . ." she begged. "I must get my letters."

The hands turned her away with force. Slumping, Katie walked down to the street where a huge crowd had gathered. She was in a trance. A familiar voice called her name and she turned, staring unseeing into the crowd. It was the cook carrying her sewing bag. He held it out proudly.

Katie wept. "Oh, Cholly—thank you. God love you." She hugged him and they both stared over at the flames engulfing their lives.

Kimball House burned for the rest of the night.

By now, the clanging of the town's engines were loud coming up Main Street followed by voices of concerned citizens who had been awakened. At the last minute the barman from the Red Dog Saloon invited everyone inside. He sent for coffee and the barmaids brought out sandwiches. The crowd was in shock. Kimball House was the core of Mesa City; they all felt an innate sadness. No one could understand where Bill Kimball was. Katie sent Cholly to tell the barman he had gone to Phoenix. They asked the telegraph operator at the train station to send a wire.

At 5 A.M. Katie and Cholly hurried into the street, still dressed in their bathrobes and slippers. Someone yelled that Kimball was riding in. Once outside they saw a lone figure on horseback poised in front of what remained of his hotel.

Bill's friends hurried toward him. Kimball stared in disbelief observing the smouldering destruction. They watched him dismount; he was devastated. Katie moved closer and put her arms around him. He patted her head softly. "That does it, Katie. I'm ruined. I can't believe it. My God! In one year's time. . . everything gone. It is hard to imagine. All the way here from Phoenix, I've thought about the reason why this would happen. I guess I'd better leave here—this place is no good for me."

He was inconsolable; Cholly and Katie stood by helplessly. Soon Kimball walked away towards the charred remains of the once beautiful building. His wife came out of the shadows and clutched him to her. They both cried. Katie turned away. "It's all done, Cholly. I've lost everything I had, too. And, if it wasn't for you, dear friend, I wouldn't have Al's letters or the photographs either."

"No, Mlissey. Cholly help. You go home. It better. This place no good for you."

"But I haven't any money, Cholly. I had it in a box in my room. It burned up. What will I do?"

The round eyes sobered, there was so much wisdom and compassion in them it brought Katie to tears. "Oh, Cholly, I can't take your money. I need clothes and a ticket to Virginia on the train. It would be impossible. I don't know when I could pay you back. Don't you see it is hopeless?"

The man suddenly smiled. "Me have money, Mlissey. Me have in bank. . . lots. . . me save long time. You no wolly. Me fix soon." He pointed to the clock on the wall above the bank.

Katie sobbed and the little Chinese cook held her for a long time. It was an awesome sight, the unlikely pair clinging together on a darkened street in front of the smoking ruin.

* * *

Two days later the minister's wife couched Katie's shoulder. "I'm sorry you're leaving, dear. We have learned to care a great deal, Katie. The town will miss you. But, after all that has happened, the pastor and I believe you are making the right decision."

"I'm indebted to you, Mrs. Carson. Thanks for offering your home. I don't know where I would have gone."

Katie was wearing a long skirted, red plaid dress with a wide black velvet ribbon around the waist. Mrs. Carson put a full length woolen cape around the girl's shoulders and watched her tie the neck cords. On her head was a matching woolen bonnet and she carried a velvet muff. She looked quite elegant. The woman remarked how beautiful she was. Laughing lightly, Katie said, "My wonderful friend, Cholly, bought everything for me. I can't believe how kind he was. He saved my life. I hope I will be able to repay him someday."

"Come, Katie. The carriage is here to take you to the station now. You don't want to miss your train," the minister called from the door of the rectory. He walked down the steps and helped her into the black cab. Katie looked back at them, she waved as the carriage rolled away. It was a last look and she wept. To get to the station they had to pass the hotel. Both driver and passenger stared in disbelief, appalled by the sight of the grotesque charred skeletal remains. The driver said, "That's a mighty big loss for Bill Kimball, he didn't deserve that. We'll lose a good man over this. . .that's for sure."

Katie's goodbys to Cholly and Bill were almost as bad as losing Senner. She wondered why life had been so ugly. It was a long way home and the thought of it did nothing to improve her emotions. There would be plenty of time to think about all that had happened. The future was very bleak.

* * *

Register of Actions

No. 8460 John Pruitt — Plaintiff | DIVISION NUMBER TWO Divorce | Sullivan & W... — Pl...

1922 Mattie Pruitt — Defendant | | Def...

DATE		PROCEEDINGS HAD	PLAINTIFF'S COSTS DR.	PLAINTIFF'S COSTS CR.	DEFENDANT DR.
April	12	Filing and docketing Complaint			
"	"	Issuing Summons & one Copy			
"	"	By Cash (Sullivan & Westervelt)		10.00	
"	15	Summons returned showing service 4/13/22			
Aug.	24	Motion and order setting for trial			
		Entg appearance pltf & dft.			
		Entg statement of counsel regarding settlement community property etc. (See Minutes)			
		Swearing Plaintiff			
		Swearing one witness for pltf			
		Cause submitted			
		Entg Judgment in favor of plaintiff			
Dec	28	By Cash Sullivan & Westervelt		5.00	
1923 Jan.	6	Filing and Docketing Judgment			
"	8	Recording Judgment			
"	8	Certificate and Final Filing of Judgment ~~in Box~~			
1928 Sep	22	Filing petition to increase alimony			
"	22	Entg & filing order to show cause			
"	22	Issuing citation			
"	25	Citation returned showing service			
Oct.	6	Swearing 5 witnesses			
"	6	Entg order directing pltf to pay to deft the sum of $50 per month & $[illegible] 80 Atty fees & costs			

Excerpt from divorce actions of John Pruitt and Mattie Pruitt.

The grounds John Pruitt used to file his divorce action against Katie were great anguish of mind, grievance, mental suffering and humiliation.

Katie's settlement was:

40 acres of land	valued at	$120.00
4 cows	valued at	100.00
4 calves	valued at	50.00
2 mares	valued at	80.00
1 mule	valued at	30.00
1 truck	valued at	100.00

— 1928

WASHINGTON AVE NORTH
From 700 E Gurley

101 City Park and Athletic Field
110 Hill Hollis W 737
112 Swift Henry L 496W
116 Hairston S J 714W
122 Goodrich Mrs Margaret o 616J
124 Olsen Raymond 1431
126 Pesnell Ray
128 Bauer Frank 266
132 Sheldon Fred J o 669W
134 Peckham Mrs Etta o
136 Barber Mrs Florence 738W
140 Taylor Joe W o 738J
201 Tharp Lloyd T o 1164R
202 Clyburn Claude 1689W
202 Bryant Paul P
206 Fotheringham Austin L 496M
207 Vacant
210 Butler Mrs Ellen o
211 McDonald Joe 728W
214 Jones Arthur
215 Bryan W J o 825J
217 Sellars Gladys o
221 Craft Leroy o 1164J
225 Kiple Jesse J o 1088W
226 Erickson Mrs Clara • 496J
230 Riley A R
233 Terrin Edward D o 1088NR
234 Hicks W E o 592R
311 Pruitt Mrs Mattie o 1164W
311½ Graham C C
315 Hubbard Byrl E o 752J
316 Vacant
317 Wagner F William 1549W

Prescott Street directory of 1953 showing Mattie Pruitt's name

Mattie Pruitt was married in Virginia in 1901 and moved to Seligman, Arizona with husband John in 1909. They later lived in Prescott. He divorced her and remarried as soon as the divorce was final.

Mattie A. Pruitt
PRESCOTT — Mrs. Mattie Ann Pruitt, 73, long-time resident of Prescott, died early Friday at a local hospital.
She was born in Franklin county, Va., and came to Seligman in 1909 and to Prescott in 1933.
Survivors include two daughters, Mrs. Mary M. Graves and Mrs. Annie Green, both of Prescott, three sons, John, Prescott; and William and George, both of Yuma; two sisters and a brother, and 10 grandchildren.
Funeral services are pending.

Mattie's obituary as it appeared in a Phoenix newspaper.

Chapter 13

Remembering

Moving from the Arizona Territory had, at first, seemed too overwhelming for Amos to contemplate. If he hadn't been so excited at the prospect of becoming a surgeon under the tutelage of the famous Dr. Marcus Wellman, the transition probably wouldn't have gone so smoothly. The thrill of realizing a lifelong dream completely captivated the man.

Once the announcement that the town's physician was leaving had been made, things began to happen. A young doctor, newly arrived in the territory, contacted Amos. Hat in hand, humbly explaining his desire to serve, the man apologized for his lack of funds. When asked about assets, he said he had a degree from a good eastern medical school. . .dedication and zeal; a beautiful young wife and a two year old son. That fact appealed to Dr. Basset. For, although Amos enjoyed Loretta Mason's elegant home, he always believed the walls should have echoed children's laughter. A deal was struck. Amos was only too happy to rent the place furnished with an option to buy if all went well. His new life did not include furniture—just two trunks full of medical books, instruments, his clothes and a small black leather pouch found in Al Senner's camp on Superstition Mountain. The letters seemed too important to leave to strangers and too precious to throw away. Standing beside the open trunk, Amos held the worn leather pouch and stared at it; indecision plagued him. Reluctantly, and grunting as he shook his lightly greying brown mane, Amos tossed it inside before closing the lid.

For the next sixteen years Doctor Amos Basset's name grew in stature among the notables of Los Angeles. He was indeed the student Dr. Wellman thought he would be. He not only studied under the man, but eventually became his partner. For the first time in his life Amos Basset enjoyed prominence and great wealth. His dedication served to occupy him totally; he remained unmarried to any woman—only medicine. And, although the sophisticated matrons of Los Angeles worked every wile, they were unable to match the handsome doctor with any eligible female of their set. The doctor remained intractable.

In 1911 Amos decided to take a well earned rest at a resort near Yuba City. One of his greatest joys was driving his new Ford along the desert roads. On the first day of his vacation he stopped at a small restaurant to have lunch. Once inside the cafe, he found a spot near the counter. He liked it because of the large window overlooking the distant mountains. That setting triggered a memory of the house in Florence as he suddenly remembered Loretta Mason's kitchen designed especially to take advantage of the view and where he had eaten contentedly. The memory surprised him. He hadn't thought of that part of his life for many years.

A black man appeared beside the counter. He smiled. "What can I do for you, Sir?"

"Soup." Amos said without looking up. "Yes, a good bowl of vegetable soup and a chicken sandwich."

"Coming right up. But, how about some coffee first?"

Amos' eyes drifted from the scenery to the man. "Yes, I'd like that."

"You like the view? That's why I built it here. It reminded me of the mountains near a place where I used to work in Arizona." He left to get the coffee.

When he returned Amos questioned him. "Where did you work in Arizona?"

"Goldfield! A mine near the Superstitions." He grinned. "I don't suppose you ever heard of it?"

"On the contrary, I know exactly where it is. I've been there."

The black man exposed a raft of pearly teeth. "No foolin'. I ain't never met anybody who knew about it. The mine played out years ago and it's a ghost town now. Excuse me, I'll go get your soup and sandwich. Be right back."

Amos' curiosity piqued. He was patient as the cook put the food in front of him. "Sit down, Sir. I'd like to ask you about Goldfield."

They were alone in the restaurant. It was pleasant.

Extending his hand, Amos introduced himself.

"Nice to meet you, Doc. My name is Baker, James Earl, but everybody calls me Trooper. I did the blasting at the mine."

"Did you ever know a highgrader named Al Senner?"

"He was no highgrader. Well, not like you is sayin'. I knew Al Senner well; we was friends. He was one of the locators of the Mammoth—he got aced out of his share. Far as I'm concerned, he only took what was his."

Amos smiled.

The black man looked puzzled. "What's that smile for?"

"I'm amazed and pleased that you actually knew Al Senner."

"Yea, I knew him until he disappeared in 1894. I guess, maybe, it was around November. I never saw him again after that. Did you know him?"

"Yes, I doctored him once when he was hurt." Amos was cautious. He didn't want to reveal very much of the story but he wanted to verify Al's words.

"Al had a girlfriend over in Mesa City who waited tables in the Kimball Hotel, her name was Katie. Everyone knew her, she was a real looker. Al promised her the moon and he meant to get it for her. And he smuggled about two pounds of ore out of that mine daily. He hand cobbed it in Goldfield wash and put the dregs into holes so, when the wash was runnin', it would disappear down stream. Then, each Saturday in the A.M. he would pack the cobbed ore up to the top of Superstition Mountain. He figured it was a hard climb and even if somebody got up there he could play tag in them rocks and boulders. Hell, I figure if he could have high-graded more than a thousand pounds of rich ore before that deputy broke his arm and ran him off the property."

"How much do you think he actually had?" Amos asked.

"At least fifteen hundred pounds. I figure he made more than twenty-five trips and he could take twenty-five pounds up each week. He did it for over a year. Okay, so maybe he didn't go up all the time. . .what difference does it make now?"

Amos learned a few more things than he originally knew. And now, he knew that Katie had worked for W.A. Kimball who owned the Pioneer Boardinghouse in Mesa City which was renamed the Kimball House when it became a hotel.

The conversation returned to Trooper's life. He made it quite clear that he had tried prospecting around Goldfield after the Mammoth closed down. He was no different than the others and when he left, he was disillusioned.

After his vacation Amos returned to Los Angeles. Marcus Wellman was very ill. As much as Amos hated to admit it, his old friend was dying and within months Amos was in practice alone. He decided to leave it that way. For thirteen more years Amos improved his considerable skills in the operating rooms of the best hospitals in Los Angeles and the surrounding areas.

On his sixty-fifth birthday, Amos Basset retired. There was a huge party and a lot of kind words; but, he longed to go back to the desert and a simpler life. He sold his home, car and most of his belongings except for two trunks which were used originally to bring him to the coast. As he packed them he encountered Al's old pouch. It seemed an omen. He sat down and opened it. The girl in the photograph stared out at him. He thought of that beautiful smile damaged when the man she loved didn't return. He thought of her pain and the fact that he had never told her what happened to Al Senner. In that moment he felt remorse as he fingered the map he had taken from the dead man's body. His eyes drifted to the few words written there. "I love Katie, this for her. Note to Bill Kimball today about will. Superstition Mountain. . .2100# $5" and underlined "$10,500" and it was signed, "Al Senner. . .1894. . .Goldfield, A.T." The initials probably stood for Arizona Territory. Amos was pensive, remembering that trip with Joe Gibson fraught with life threatening experiences. He shook his head and putting the documents and photograph back inside the pouch, Amos laid the case into his trunk. What a strange turn of events. Doctor Amos Basset had lived a lifetime in Los Angeles; he had been there for thirty-one years. Now, it seemed he was being drawn back to Arizona and another world he barely remembered.

As fate would have it, Amos arrived in Arizona in April, the same month that he left. The desert was blooming and ablaze with color. He marveled at its beauty as he rolled along on the the Union Auto Stage Line towards his destination. It was 1925. The bus stopped in Mesa and Amos stepped off it. His eyes toured the sight of a city completely changed by the passage of so much time and for a long while he just drank in the view.

Within a few days he had rented an apartment on east Main Street and purchased a car. The luxury of having as much time as he needed appealed to the man. His winning personality opened doors and gave him answers to a lot of questions. Of course, first on his agenda was the Kimball Hotel. He reasoned that someone there might know an old employee or might have some records regarding Katie. When he inquired, most people didn't really respond, difficult though it was, it had been thirty-one years. Eventually, he met an old woman who ran the newstand on the corner near his hotel.

"Say Mam, would you happen to know anything about an old hotel called the Pioneer or Kimball House?" he asked after he purchased the paper.

She smiled softly. "Why yes, I do. It burned down in 1900. Poor old Bill Kimball lost his shirt. Funny about him, you know, he owned the livery, the stage line to Goldfield and Government Wells and Phoenix from Mesa City. He owned a saloon and a hotel in Goldfield and the Pioneer which was rebuilt earlier and renamed the Kimball House. He was a good man, too. I mean he helped everybody and the people who worked for him really liked him. Why do you ask?"

"Oh, I was seeking information about a woman who worked for him there. Her name was Katie. Did you know her?"

"No, I don't think I did. But, I didn't come to Mesa City until the year it burned. My husband was a miner out at Goldfield. When it closed we were broke. They were very trying times, I'll tell you. A lot of folks left here then. There wasn't any work."

Amos thanked her, took his paper and left.

At the tack and feed store on the far end of town he learned that a man named William A. Barkley now owned the old Marler Ranch where Joe Gibson had worked. The sound of that name brought a flood of memories back into his conscious mind as he remembered the thrill of climbing those sheer cliffs on a horse in ice and snow. For a second he actually shivered as he relived the cold. He pictured Joe Gibson in the old brown chaps throwing a lasso across the roaring arroya to help him cross. Those memories raised a satisfied smile. Amos would never have learned of Al Senner's fate without the cowboy's knowledge and experience. Instantly, he decided to find Barkley and ask about Joe. He looked satisfied approaching the clerk, then mentioned the Barkley ranch saying he had been out there years ago. Just as he was about to ask specific directions, Barkley came into the mercantile. The clerk pointed him out.

Barkley was friendly, even inviting the newcomer out to the ranch for a visit.

Amos drove out there on the following weekend as they planned. The house was comfortable and there was a cold lunch waiting on the table. Remembering Joe Gibson drawing iced well water, Amos asked for some. It still tasted good; he savored it.

During the visit, Amos learned that Joe Gibson had moved on. They thought he was on a ranch near Wickenburg but no one knew for certain. Barkley was looking for the Lost Dutchman's mine and he had plenty to say about that lost treasure,in fact, he had assumed the doctor was on that same quest. He joked about it. Amos shook his head. "No, I was offered a proposition on some property in Goldfield. I turned it down."

"And, well you should." The rancher answered. "That mine is played out for real. Only in the early days did they ever hit it big in Goldfield."

Out of curiosity the doctor inquired as to trails up the main Superstition Mountain. Barkley said there really weren't any. He said that cattle often wandered up there but didn't stay long because only after storms was there any water up on top.

After a satisfying lunch, Amos thanked his host and left. On the drive back he thought of how futile a trip up to the top of the mountain might be for someone his age. He didn't need money. At that moment he decided he was more interested in the people Al Senner knew than in the gold. Of course, the fact that Amos Basset had made money helped.

For the next weeks the doctor wandered about the town looking for old timers who might have remembered the people who worked in Kimball's Hotel. Later in the month, as he rested in the park, Amos made the acquaintance of an old Chinese man named Cholly. Again the doctor asked if he knew many people who had lived in the town in the late 1800's. Cholly grinned knowingly. "Les. . . I did."

Dr. Basset's frame stiffened. "You did? That's wonderful. I'm trying to find out about Bill Kimball and the people who worked in his hotel."

"Me worked 'Klimball House'." His grin widened and a toothless space was exposed in his mouth. His skin drew taut over the round face and he giggled nervously as if he was pleased to have the chance to talk about it.

"Did you ever know a woman named Katie? She was in love

with a cowboy named Al Senner."

"Me know her. She velly' pletty', 'Mlissey. She velly' nice. Too blad', cowboy no come back. She cly' all time."

Amos' heart was racing. He could not believe his good fortune. He took a deep breath before asking the next question.

"Do you know what happened to her?"

Cholly smiled broadly. "Oh, les', hotel burn down. Long time ago. Me cook, me go restaurant. Mlissey' Katie she go back home."

"Where?"

"Me tink East—unhuh—unhuh, les'."

The doctor's face drooped. Cholly stared at him.

"Me know some more." He grinned his toothless look which had become inscrutable.

"What?" He said in a raised, almost impatient tone.

"She come 'black. She on ranch 2 mile east." Cholly giggled.

"Thank you, Cholly. You have been a great help. Oh, is she married?"

Cholly shrugged unknowingly.

The trip out to the ranch seemed endless; suddenly, Amos was excited. In his mind's eye was the girl in the tin-type. Momentarily he forgot that thirty-one years had passed and he became agitated as if he were rushing to see someone he'd known for a long time.

A typical white clapboard house sat neatly in a fenced yard at the end of a long dirt road bordered on either side by flat, neatly planted cottonfields. Off in the distance Amos could see the giant Superstition Range. He thought it appropriate that he could see them on this special day. As he drove in, he was struck by trees with profuse foliage swaying gently around the house's white perimeter, excluding the sun's glare under an umbrella of green. The scene appeared tranquil and welcoming. Climbing out of the Ford, the doctor straightened his tie before opening the gate. At the door he paused to clear his throat; then, rang the doorbell. When she opened the door he gasped. She the three hour hike to the summit of Superstition Mountain. He usually carried between 10 and 15 pounds of the richest ore imaginable. Of course during the summer months he did not make trips to the top of the Mountain. The debris which was left he cleverly buried in Goldfield Wash, then during flash floods it was carried away leaving no evidence of his operation. Al knew there was no safe places around Goldfield to cache his ore and hikes into the surrounding desert by miners ~~were~~ closely scrutinized by mine officials.

He realized few would attempt to follow him to the top of Superstition Mountain and if they did he could easily elude them in the maze of rocks on top. Within seven months he had more than 400 pounds of high-grade ore cached high upon Superstition Mountain. Al continued his high grading throughout the ~~summer~~ winter of 1893-94. Carl estimated Al highgraded close to 1500 lbs of rich ore before the fateful day in November of 1894 when the deputy broke his arm.

Carl assured the doctor Al confided in no one and had never drawn map as to the location of his high grade cache. Now the doctor was positive Al Senner had hidden a large cache, much larger then he originally thought.

Page out of Tom Kollenborn's diary corroborating the doctor's visit with the man from Tuba City who worked in Goldfield with Al Senner.

was fifty years old chronologically but her face belied the passage of time; she looked forty. Her hair was darker than he'd imagined and it was tied into a knot on the top of her head. There were traces of gray in the wisps that had escaped from the knot. They hung softly around her beautiful face. Her eyes were clear and kind and Amos was at a loss for words. Seeing his discomfort, she said, "Yes, may I help you?"

He felt foolish. In a moment he regained control and said, "Are you Katie?"

"Why, yes?" Her frown exposed the bewilderment she was experiencing. The man looked proper and dignified—yet he seemed confused.

"I'd like to talk to you."

The woman appeared curious but was polite, even patient. "I'm busy right now but I will be free at eight o'clock. If you'd care to wait?"

"Yes. I'll take a ride in my car and come back for you." He watched as she turned to go back inside.

At eight P.M. she emerged carrying a purse and a wrap. She opened the car door and told him he could drive her to her home and they could visit there. It was several miles away, on the edge of town.

Once they arrived, Katie climbed out and said, "Why are you interested in me?"

"It isn't exactly you I'm interested in . . . it is Al Senner. Wasn't he your boyfriend years ago?"

"What do you know about Al?" she said with suspicion. "He disappeared and that was a life-time ago. I waited for him to return," she seemed suddenly sad . . . "Imagine that was thirty-one years ago." Katie appeared contrite until a swell of anger raised. "If you are going to talk about his supposed illegal activities you can get in your car and leave now." She lifted her long skirt and started up onto her porch. There was determination in her gait and the Doctor realized he hadn't handled things well.

"No, please, wait. I have very important information for you concerning Al and I believe there is something we should share because of it. First of all, I am only interested in proving Al's innocence of any wrong-doing at Goldfield thirty-one years ago."

Katie stopped. Her grave look became inquisitive before she spoke. "After all these years, why would you be interested in proving or disproving accusations made that long ago?"

"May I come inside where we can sit and talk?"

She nodded and went to unlock the door of the modest dwelling. It was white clapboard sitting in a sea of flowers. The scent coming from the blooms became sweet. After a few minutes, Amos sniffed and coughed. He had always been allergic to certain plants. In his haste to go inside he forgot about the scent but pulled out a handkerchief and blew his nose before entering. He followed, waiting while she lit a lamp against the fading light. The room was cosy and comfortable. Katie motioned him to a comfortable chair. She went to the kitchen and returned with hot tea and some cookies which she placed on a table between them. Amos nodded and smiled his appreciation as she poured him a cup.

Katie remained silent. If she was apprehensive it didn't show.

"Al Senner was one of my patients."

"I don't believe you." It was said in a matter-of-fact tone.

Amos pleaded, "Please, just listen." He began with finding Al in the front yard and talked about the amputation and their friendship. It was quite dark outside when he concluded. He looked at the woman who sat mute staring into space beside him.

"But, why wouldn't he come to me for consolation? He knew I loved him. I just don't understand that."

The doctor explained what happens to men who are not whole anymore. Katie seemed suddenly bereft, not listening, as though she had gone to a place where he could not follow. He was experiencing some remorse but realized that it was finally completed. Amos sighed. They were quiet momentarily. Finally, he said, "Did Al send you any letters from Goldfield?"

Katie thought of the packet in her trunk, now yellow with age. "Just some notes. Nothing of any consequence." She didn't want to explain that Al could barely read or write.

Amos cleared his throat. "Katie, Al Senner died in the Superstition Mountains in the winter of 1895. I was there. I am the doctor who certified his death certificate in Pinal County. He fell from the top of a high cliff in the Superstitions while packing gold ore. I found his body and I buried him."

As he concluded, Amos watched her. There were no tears, just relief. The beautiful face seemed relaxed and the previous tension drained away.

"The news is bad, Doctor Basset, but at least you've freed me of an old pain. All these years I expected him to return; I've waited for such a long time but eventually I gave up hope. Now, you've changed all of that. . .I'm free at last. You have given me a new life. . .thank you."

Again Amos questioned her about receiving anything from Al Senner. She got up and went into another room. Returning, Katie handed him a tin-type. It was picture of the Superstition Mountain which was signed by Al Senner. It was sent from Florence, Arizona in the winter of 1895. Amos examined the writing. It said, "See you soon, Love Al."

Getting up slowly, Katie looked at him. "If you'd like to have that, you are welcome." Her voice was soft, coaxing—he wanted to get up and put his arms around her.

Doctor Basset started to refuse but reconsidering, smiled lazily, and put it into his pocket on his way to the front door.

"I think you deserve that. You certainly did a lot for Al and now for me. I'm very grateful to you."

"There is something else you need to know, Katie. Al Senner had a map on his body when I found it. He wrote on it that it was for you. He said he intended to make a will and had written a sum on it and signed his name and the date. I never found his gold but he was definitely sincere in his wish for you to have it."

Katie's smile was enigmatic. The doctor would never know how desperate she had been many times. It seemed an irony that neither of them ever had the gold. In that instant she wondered if she had actually killed Al Senner by asking for too much.

On the drive home Amos reconsidered the evidence. It didn't seem possible that no one knew where Senner hid the gold. The man must have been so confident that nothing would happen to him that he just didn't record it. He went to sleep that night, and many after that, pondering the puzzle.

Amos spent a lot of sleepless nights before making a decision. He was too old to go into the Superstitions looking for treasure but if he couldn't have Senner's gold, maybe he could have Senner's woman.

In 1925 the summer was exceptionally hot. While living in Los Angeles Amos had forgotten about the desert heat. He decided to move off the desert for the summer and go up into the cooler climate available in the mountains to the north. It seemed reasonable to say goodby to Katie. Amos drove out to her home around dusk one evening, she was sitting on the porch. He saw her beautiful face brighten as he drove in.

"It's been awhile," Amos said as he approached. It had been four weeks exactly. It might as well have been a life-time.

"Yes, please come on up and sit down. Would you like a cold drink?"

The doctor seemed preoccupied. He didn't answer her, instead he blurted out, "Katie, I have a question to ask you."

The woman sobered and looked expectant.

"Would you like to work for me? I'll provide you with anything you like: a nice home, an estate after my death. . .I need you. . .and I want to take care of you for the rest of your life."

"Is this a proposal, Doctor?"

"Take it any way you like it, Katie. I'd like to make you happy."

"I'll accept whatever terms you wish, my good doctor. I

wasn't certain you would ever return but I was waiting. I have been alone and lonely for a long time but there are things you don't know about me."

"I don't care what you've done, Katie. All I know is, I'd like to share my life with you and I feel as though I know you and have for half a life-time." He stood up and approached her, drawing her onto her feet. He put his arms around her and held her close. Katie's sigh was all the answer he needed and when he kissed her he knew why he had waited all of these years.

Then, he reached inside his jacket and withdrew a packet of letters which he handed to her. Amos smiled—"No, I never read them, Katie."

Chapter 14

The Information

When Tom Kollenborn gave any credence to Katie's story, she was already dead. The diaries his father meticulously kept were put into the family garage by his mother shortly after his father's death in 1961. A torrential rain storm flooded the area and Tom's legacy was soaked. By the time Kollenborn realized where by were, it was too late; much of the information his father recorded had been lost forever. He took the material in hand and tried to translate what was left on pages which were not stuck together or water stained. The pair had taken regular trips into the Superstitions from the time Tom was a young boy, gaining knowledge and having the ultimate father and son experience. George Kollenborn was a mining engineer. He had much to pass on to his son plus the love of the lore and an insatiable curiosity which inevitably led them both up (just one more canyon). His dedication to their search had resulted in the precious journals, some of which were now destroyed.

Tom eventually became a geologist, which gave him a new perpective on the area. He had also been a cowboy for several years until a bull gored him and his friend, Tex Barkley, convinced him "punchin' cows was not for him." New searches ultimately led to discoveries formally written about by George Kollenborn; some were vaguely remembered. He still searched for things which had eluded both men, especially the location of the Lost Dutchman's Mine. As his interest in the Superstitions became a major factor in his life and following his father's lead, he regularly recorded his own trips into the range.

Tom's most satisfying experience was saddling his horse, Crow, and going up the canyons accompanied by Duke, his dog. For many years to come, both animals would be his constant companions. Tom's youth had been spent as a wrangler. It is an accepted fact—cowboys won't go anywhere they can't take a horse. They rarely dismount, and then only to tie up a calf, aid a sick animal or bed down for the night. Tom was no exception. Duke, who Tom rattlesnake trained by tying a dead rattler around his throat, hated the scent. Tom could sleep anywhere in that unpredictable terrain without fear of man or beast. No snake would crawl close to Tom's campfire without Duke's undivided attention: he would pounce upon the snake, shake it senseless and then, tear it to pieces. In fact, Duke had been known to take the front off of the jacket of any interloper who dared approach Tom's camp uninvited. The man was definitely safe and he and the animals inseparable.

Tom's photography became an avocation as more and more people were interested: not only in the famed Lost Dutchman's Mine, but in the Superstition Range itself. Later, there would be numerous requests from civic organizations, schools and private groups to hear Tom's stories, told in an interesting manner accompanied by the colorful slides.

Early in 1980, Tom Kollenborn had already become friendly with another Dutchman hunter, Arizona's Attorney General, Bob Corbin. Since the pair rode into the Superstitions frequently, it became their norm to share stories around the campfire at night. They were both avid readers as well as collectors of legends. Corbin also had been studying archaeology and history for many years; there was no chance of boredom, the pair had plenty to talk about. Each had theories regarding the history of the range, the trappers and Indian fighters and the prospectors and miners of the early West. Of course, Kollenborn was also a geologist and had written several books. Their conversations were stimulating as well as informative; and, each man looked forward to their trips which were by now well known statewide. Because of their knowledge and titles, the press frequently did stories about them. There had been national magazine and newspaper articles, even local television stories and one national television show done by *Unsolved Mysteries*, which would be rerun many times. Everyone sought them out. People from all walks of life fairly begged to be taken along—but the pair knew company would only slow them down. It took a long time to get to the sites they wanted to investigate. This wasn't a weekend outing; this was serious business and they had no intention of sharing their secrets.

Tom was a teacher. He taught in Apache Junction High School and later, he became an administrator in the school district. Living close to those mountains and the stable was a personal choice, allowing him accessibility for spontaneous trips. Bob Corbin, on the other hand, was totally involved in a political career; he had precious little time to enjoy their much coveted treks into the Superstitions. He also lived many miles away from the range; therefore, having once planned such an event, the lawman was firm in his resolve to go.

Shortly thereafter, Tom was invited to a town in southern Arizona to do a slide show. Just after finishing his presentation, he began collecting his gear to pack into the truck. Someone said hello. An elderly woman approached him to ask if he and his partner, Bob Corbin, would be interested in a diary and a treasure map she accidently found in the bottom of an inherited trunk of medical books. Tom nodded. The statement was definitely a surprise. She said it was generally known the pair were honest and dependable and she was too old to go looking for gold. The lady decided to trust them. Tom's interest piqued. After an invitation he followed her to her home. She was quick to inform Tom the matter had to be kept in the strictest confidence and swore him to secrecy. Tom, being a man of his word, agreed. Her plan was to expect a fifty-fifty split if—as a result of her map—they actually found the treasure. The whole situation seemed intriguing; a bargain was struck and Kollenborn sat down to read the diary.

After a cursory examination of the book, he learned the author, a doctor, had been a soldier in the Territory of Arizona during the end of the Apache wars and had mustered out in the late 1800's to take a job at the Silver King Mine. Eventually, he opened a practice in Florence, Arizona. After amputating the arm of a miner named Al Senner, who worked in Goldfield, the doctor grubstaked the miner to retrieve a large cache from Superstition Mountain. The miner never returned. Doctor Basset decided to hunt for the man; he feared the worst. He hired cowboy Joe Gibson to take him up onto the main mountain in search of 1000 pounds of cobbed Goldfield ore which Senner had stolen for love of a woman named Katie. Fate brought the two men to the death site of the unfortunate miner. There the doctor put together a hasty grave and said a few prayers. Thirty years later, after a successful career as a surgeon in Los Angeles, the doctor returned to search for Katie. He asked her to come and be his housekeeper and offered to care for her any way she wanted it. They never married but were together until 1949 when the doctor died.

As Kollenborn read the notes he thought they had a familiar ring. He was puzzled. Where had he heard this story before? It was late. Tom excused himself, thanked the lady and left with her promise he could return again. All the way home he was troubled by the facts as presented. It was not an ordinary story. A week later on the drive to work, he remembered that time so long ago, when he was fifteen and his father had been hurt in an automobile accident. George was seriously hurt. Their family moved to Prescott in order for his Dad to receive medical care at Fort Whipple Veteran's Hospital. Tom grinned. Suddenly, he remembered Katie. At least, he remembered an elderly neighbor with whom he and his father, George Kollenborn, had become acquainted when they lived on Washington Street that summer. Tom mowed her lawn, after which she would give them lemonade. During those pleasant interludes, she related the story of Al Senner, and the doctor, Amos Basset, whom she said she had loved until his death in 1949. When Tom said the Superstitions were cursed, Katie replied, "Oh! No, those mountains brought me my wonderful doctor." Tom was remembering the incident, but it had been over 30 years. Certainly any story about treasure was fixed into his brain but exact names and dates escaped him. Later, he said her name was Katie Green—then, he remembered the name Annie Green. Finally, after a good long memory search he said, KATIE ANN PRUITT, and he told Bob Corbin he was certain that was her name. (Legal documents show Annie Green owned the house his father rented. According to a relative, Annie Green was Katie Pruitt's daughter. Mattie Pruitt was listed in the street directory and the local phone book at the same address, 311 North Washington Street in 1952-53. Her obituary gave her name as Mattie Ann Pruitt age 78. There were numerous legal documents in the county court house proving her existence. Obviously, the lady preferred to be called Katie in her youth. That was not uncommon among the transient population of the Territory. It isn't relevant. Tom wrote her name down and gave it to Bob to give to me. It was Katie Ann Pruitt; the obituary gave her name as Mattie Ann Pruitt. One would doubt they are not one-and-the-same given the evidence. There are also divorce papers and a long record of legal battles involving Katie or Mattie's children, three of whom were put into an orphanage in Prescott. The complaint alleged that "Mattie was an elderly woman of 55 years of age who earned her livelihood as a domestic when able to secure employment and (who has no funds with which to secure counsel to defend the action.)"

(Those documents attest to the fact the lady was a housekeeper, as she was alleged to have been when the doctor returned in 1925 looking for her.)

Tom Kollenborn examining the map.

Bob Corbin riding into Superstition Mountains—1985.

Tom returned to southern Arizona to ask if he could see the diary again. As he thumbed through it, a folded sheet fell out. Tom retrieved it and flipped it open—it was the map, hand drawn and signed by Al Senner with writing on it. On one end was a statement by the doctor saying he had taken the map from Al Senner's body on Superstition Mountain in 1895. He asked for permission to copy the map; it was granted.

Naturally, Tom was anxious to arrange a trip with his friend, Bob Corbin. This time the story around the campfire would be really exciting. But, more than the story was the actual map drawn by Katie's lover. Bob had been busy campaigning and was unable to go until after November.

Tom, eager to locate the trail, spent a long time on his horse covering the vast area which spread around the base of the mountain. He hoped to find a beaten track leading to Senner's cache. Normally, Senner climbed up Siphon Draw on foot, but he had said there was a trail which took a day to get to on horseback. That search took him months. Eventually, a helicopter pilot he knew offered to fly him over the top and the perimeters of the main mountain. They made the trip many times but to no avail. The ex-cowboy followed some game trails which looked promising but they always came to a dead end before reaching the bottom. Finally in desperation, Tom forged a new trail which switchbacked to the mesa.

In December of 1985, Tom Kollenborn and his friend, Bob Corbin, planned a trip to the top of Superstition Mountain. This was Corbin's initial trip, one Tom had already made many times. He had located the areas marked on the map; unfortunately, there was no gold. The most difficult task had been finding the gravesite. Eventually, he found it in a place called Flat Iron Canyon which is sandwiched between Monument Canyon and Hog Canyon. It took much longer to locate the skeleton. After a long climb and a good search he found Senner's badly decomposed remains right where the doctor said he buried it. All of the bones were there with the exception of the left arm below the elbow.

Tom replaced everything, covered the grave with rocks and left a marker by it for identification. (That marker has been removed by someone). He stated it was about 800 feet from the top of the mesa, wedged against the side of the mountain in a canyon which was on the southside of the western end of Superstition Mountain.

Tom explained to Bob how little water there was on top and in order to have sufficient for their horses, especially after such a hard climb, they would need to make the trek in winter or just after the rains. It was now December.

They could not attempt to go up on the west side of Superstition Mountain which is nearly straight up and the exact place, Siphon Draw, which Senner had climbed on foot. The south and the east side of the main mountain had as many pitfalls as the west. They discussed it at length. Bob didn't question the wisdom of Tom's experience. The lawyer could ride and felt quite comfortable doing so, but his lifestyle prohibited any regular experience in the saddle. Tom explained that by now he had made a trail and they would follow that one.

Corbin left the following evening and drove to Apache Junction. It was expedient for him to spend the night at Kollenborn's house in order to leave just before sun-up and be on the trail early. They kept the horses quartered at Ron & Jane Feldman's O K Corral, west of Goldfield. The trip from Tom's home to the stables took about a half an hour. They saddled up and left just as the main mountain, due east, lit from behind by the promise of a glorious new day.

The corral was deserted. They both loved this particular time when the new light was still trapped behind the giant mountain. The ride zig-zagged through shadow bathed cactus and the palo verdes hung still in the soft grey dawn. It was cold. A few birds sang as they moved across the stillness surrounding the trail and the horses snorted smoke from flaring nostrils.

In the beginning they rode off the Apache Trail on the road to First Water and then turned east towards Weaver's Needle.

Up ahead the giant spire was imposing. No one who saw it remained unaffected. They watched it grow in stature as the sunrise raised above it. Continuing for about three miles to the second pass, their horses turned onto a narrow, barely discernable trail and headed into West Boulder Canyon. It seemed practical to rest at a running stream. Shortly, the animals suckled the cool, clear water. Everyone knew the danger of the trail and the possibility that there might be very little water up above. Bob mounted his horse following Tom's lead. They were headed to a place where West Boulder Canyon and Old West Boulder Canyon intersect and had made good time. The sun wasn't very high yet, and each man knew it would take at least five hours to mount the summit during a very dangerous climb.

Bob said they started up the steep sides and then, shortly turned right towards the west. Moving slowly, through loose shale along the north side of the main mountain, the party eventually reached the half way mark. That part of the trip was perilous. Bob climbed out of the saddle a few times, to avoid being on the horse when he jumped across a place which was hazardous. He could see the broken pieces of shale constantly dislodging, which could be heard slamming against the mountain, as they fell hundreds of feet below. Occasionally, the cowboy did the same. The trail was treacherous and unforgiving.

They were now in the middle of the sheer east side. Tom advised they turn west once they were on top which took better than two hours to accomplish. At the crest the riders continued toward the extreme west end of Superstition Mountain. The three pine trees came into view. Bob knew the trees were markers on the map, he grinned. They were now almost into the exact location of Senner's camp.

Riding in elicited a few sighs. How rewarding to be on the top viewing extraordinary sights out in the distance and knowing this was actually the place where the cowboy had been 100 years ago. Both men appreciated history, experiencing some ethereal reward for achieving the difficult geographic locations of men who came before.

Corbin examined the map in detail once he was allowed to see it. Naturally, he carefully searched all of the spots marked. The place seemed unlike any other they had seen. The top of the main mountain might be likened to a moonscape. There are huge boulders and clumps of pock marked basalt with indentations the size of deep bowls. The mounds of earth smoothed into layers stairstepped in places until they reached the rocks. Fortunately, there had been recent rains and the pot holes were flush with fresh water for their animals. Dismounting, they made camp and gave the animals a chance to be free of their saddles. They would happily graze on available grass until later when the men would give them grain carried up by the pack animal.

There was an extraordinary view of Phoenix off to the west and Mesa to the south. Bob walked to the edge of the precipice where Al Senner had lost his life. He thought of the sense of history there—one could feel it. Tom approached, pointing to the ledge. It was a sheer drop of over 800 feet down into Flat Iron Canyon, a place named by Tom.

"No one could survive a fall below, Bob," Tom said.

Bob shook his head. He could not see the gravesite and asked about it. Tom explained that it was beneath a ledge and not visible from the cliff.

Later, after exploring for awhile, they cooked supper. It was getting late and the men were tired; it had been a long day. Soon it was dark. They walked to the western edge where they could clearly see Goldfield as Senner must have done. It seemed strange to be standing in his footsteps. 'Too bad,' Bob thought, 'Why didn't he make a record of his movements off this mountain?'

They built up the fire against the cold night. Their sleeping bags were welcomed and still the conversation went on until late. The puzzle intrigued both men. It seemed reasonable to conclude maps are rarely accurate, especially hand drawn ones.

They made allowances for every eventuality probably considered by Senner and the Doctor. The two men were tired and their sleep on the wind chilled mesa was deep and dreamless. For several days every avenue was explored but to no avail, there just wasn't a cache to be found anywhere. Soon it was time to return to town. If they were reluctant it was momentary, each knowing there was a lot to rethink and many more trips to make both by helicopter and on horseback. Another mystery had been presented but it intrigued and challenged them.

Much later, Tom Kollenborn checked the records of the Quarter Circle U Ranch and found out that Joe Gibson had worked for Marler, the owner late in the 1800's. A newspaper article is included which will verify Joe Gibson's existence. Tom took a photograph of Al Senner's grave which he says has been lost or stolen from his collection. He and Bob Corbin spent hours going through the photographs and some 3500 slides without locating it. Suffice to say, the grave is there, remnants of a human being whose story would have remained unknown but for a quirk of fate.

Corbin said he made the trip probably five or six times. He is satisfied that he and Tom have covered the site. Both men had heard stories of float ore being found in Old West Boulder Canyon. No one can remember the time sequence. Al Senner was definitely taking his gold off the mountain when he was killed. Certainly, it is reasonable to assume he stashed it in Old West Boulder Canyon. Given the terrain and the long climb, up or down, why wouldn't he put it there? More than one source claimed Senner was the possessor of over 1000 pounds of cobbed ore. The map offers Al's signature and statements regarding his love for Katie. He wrote of a need to draft a will which would leave her $10,500 dollars. Now, of course, for the big question. Where is his cache? It seems uncanny that Senner would have removed all of his stash and on the final trip been sent careening over the cliff to his death. Naturally, stranger things have happened. If he rode off the mountain by a trail, the winds of time have destroyed it, but, more than likely, the cache was hidden close to that trail. The stories of float ore being found in Old West Boulder Canyon could verify the rest of the story. Senner only had one arm. He was probably returning from taking the ore off the mountain with a pack mule when he was killed. That means he might have gone down the way Tom and Bob did. And, of course, if he believed the trip to be a fleeting experience—he wouldn't have hidden it very well—thinking he would be right back to claim it. The map in his pocket was of the hiding place on the top of the main mountain, which he had probably stripped of its treasure by the time he was killed. He was definitely coming back to the camp. He would never have left the mule tethered knowing it would die, nor would he have left Katie's letters or his rifle.

Tom and Bob searched for a long time. They rehashed the clues over and over trying to fathom the mystery. What remains is another lost Superstition treasure. For some unknown reason those canyons clutch their gold tenaciously. Anyone who actually finds ore seems to have a difficult time keeping it. There was tragedy surrounding the ore, but certainly, intrigue and mystery laced the fabric of each of their lives. Well, treasure seeker . . . here are the facts as we know them.

Five miles north of Apache Junction, Arizona is a replica of a town called Goldfield, built by Bob Shoose several years ago. It is not your usual tourist mecca. It looks real—much the same as the original town whose ruins are a few miles north and east. Under the streets of both places are miles of tunnels Al Senner and Trooper actually worked, exactly 100 years ago. One should go there in the pale of dusk when the soft breezes are swaying through the palo verde trees and climb up the long wood steps to the weathered board restaurant to have a refreshing drink. Out on a splinter surfaced porch, it is possible to enjoy purple and fuchsia shadows silently slipping across the face of the main mountain, due east. One will not forget the view. From this place the indomitable Superstition Mountain's majesty is evident. But, more than the beauty, this view exposes the route Senner took up Siphon Draw. Then, and only then, one can really appreciate the tenacity of men like Al Senner, Joe Gibson and Doc Basset, and the present day gold seekers, Tom Kollenborn and Bob Corbin. There aren't many who would attempt that climb. Going up on top takes courage and conviction and a dedication to one's beliefs; but one needs to see the place to realize what they accomplished. Perhaps, as the viewer looks out into the desert where the old Goldfield can still be seen, imagining Senner making his weekly climb up that fierce trail, one could feel empathy for the miner cowboy who gave up his life for gold.

As I've said before in other books. . .searching for treasure is for the fearless unless one is satisfied to have their adventures vicariously by reading about it. ENJOY. . . .

Helen Corbin

—ORDER FORM—

For additional copies of *Senner's Gold* or Author Corbin's previous titles, fill out form below and mail or fax to Foxwest Publishing Co.

THE CURSE OF THE
DUTCHMAN'S
GOLD

Containing new evidence and maps providing the existence of Arizona's most cryptic lost mine.

237 Pages

The adventures of Alaska's most famous living bush pilot, Don Johnson. The result of six years of interviews on the Alaskan mainland and the Aleutian chain.

296 Pages

Please enclose check for $12.95 plus $2.50 each for tax, postage and handling in the U.S.

	QTY	$ AMOUNT
The Curse of the Dutchman's Gold		
King of the Ice		
Senner's Gold		
TOTAL		

Fill out and mail to:

Foxwest Publishing Co.
Executive Offices
2834 N. 29th St.
Suites 1-3
Phoenix, AZ 85008

PLEASE PRINT

NAME ____

ADDRESS ____

CITY ____

STATE ______________________________ ZIP____________